I Forgive You

D.C. Page

Copyright © 2024 D.C. Page
All rights reserved
First Edition

PAGE PUBLISHING
Conneaut Lake, PA

First originally published by Page Publishing 2024

ISBN 979-8-88960-171-5 (pbk)
ISBN 979-8-88960-180-7 (digital)

Printed in the United States of America

To my father, Charles David Page.
Cover photo: Sgt. Charles Page, Army 1941

Contents

Foreword vii
Acknowledgments ix
Special Thanks xi

The Book of Life 1
The Parades 3
Army Physical 8
Graduation 14
The Plane 18
Haircut 22
Syracuse Sidewalk 28
The Trip South 39
Daytona Beach 48
Post Trip 55
A Different Kind of Road Trip 62
The Interview 69
The Job 73
Big Mistake 79
School 86
Being a Coward 95
End of the Tour 104

The Uniform 109
Overboard 119
Crossing the State Line 126

Epilogue 129

Foreword

Life is like a parade. Sometimes we are in the parade, and sometimes we are on the side of the street, watching it go by. There are times when the center of attraction is so incredibly intense that it demands to be viewed again and again, even when in reality that section of the parade has passed. This book is about such an occasion, when the parade kept marching in place, preventing the next act from taking its rightful place. Post-traumatic stress disorder is real. It is horrifying. It is misunderstood, underdiagnosed, and often untreated.

Approximately six out of every one hundred people will have PTSD in the US during a given year, according to the National Center for PTSD.

About eight million people are affected by PTSD worldwide, and one in thirteen people will develop PTSD at some point in their lifetime.

The causes of post-traumatic stress disorder are numerous and include the following:

- Serious accidents
- Physical or sexual abuse
- Abuse, including childhood or domestic abuse

- Exposure to traumatic events
- Serious health problems
- Childbirth experiences
- Combat exposure

This book tells the true story of PTSD as the result of combat exposure. I am sharing my personal experiences and observations because my goal is to make more people aware of this illness and to encourage those who are suffering to seek professional help.

Recovery is possible.

Acknowledgments

I want to thank my wife, Terry, our children, Mary Mooney, Robert Filice, and all who support my creative efforts.

Special Thanks

To the professionals, loved ones, and friends who treat and support those suffering from post-traumatic stress disorder.

The Book of Life

There are those who enter your life's story and stay for a while, radically altering the direction of the plot, affecting attitudes, emotions, and actions of other characters. Such was the case with the character who tried to kill me!

Lots of people come into each person's life and everyone has an effect on the multiple stories that become your life's book.

Some of these characters stay for just a few minutes and are gone, like a waitress who breezes in and out, leaving barely a trace behind, like the aroma of the hot coffee she serves.

Life's book is filled with words spoken to meet the prompt of a previous set of words. It is also filled with actions and reactions as we move and adjust to current circumstances. We do the best we can, considering the fact that all we have to rely on are yesterday's chapters, intuition, and rumors.

Each character speaks words made up in the moment in a setting appropriate to the time and space, with a plot determined by circumstances which may be beyond anyone's control. Their motivation can be based on facts, fears, fantasies, or all three.

Some characters become best friends, while others become enemies. Some are invited in, and some force their way. Some are seen as teammates, work colleagues, or comrades with shared interests and common goals or orders. Some we love and some we don't. Some come to help or heal, and some come to hurt. Some come to give, and some come to take. Some we want close, but they're not. Some we don't want close, but they are. Some we only see from a distance. Some we walk with in silence. Some we hold hands with and talk. Some we wrestle with, and with some, we dance.

I have lived many years and have interacted with multiple thousands of people in all kinds of ways, under different situations. I look for stories within my own life to which I have the best view and firsthand knowledge. This is one of them.

This true story is based on people whose paths I crossed. Some are minor characters, but all are necessary to properly tell the story they were a part of.

A writer must have a chemist's eye, staying alert when personalities are added to the mix resulting in change. Change is always at the heart of every story. I have documented the actions and reactions that I not only witnessed but also experienced, for I am in the mix as a major character in this story.

Writing about one's own life mandates honest reflection, and that is hard work! It requires reliving the past and examining every detail. More than once, I threw my hands up, saying, "I can't do this," but I did! The process took me to a place of many questions, a few answers, and an opportunity to let go of something I'd grown weary of carrying.

The Parades

I grew up in Mattydale, New York. It was a sleepy small town a few miles outside Syracuse, which is a good-sized city.

Mattydale and the entire area grew rapidly following the end of World War II. Farm fields became housing developments almost overnight. Main Street was lined with huge elm trees along with the same businesses that could be found in every small town across the United States. There was the post office, the bank, movie theater, a number of different churches, one elementary school, a doctor's office, a dentist's office, barbershop, and a firehouse. There also was a family-run grocery store, two gas stations, two dairies, a couple of five-and-dime stores, a dress shop, and a library. I mustn't forget to mention the hardware store, ice cream shop, bar, and funeral home.

I could ride my bicycle through the center of town and not see a single car. It was a great place to grow up, and the town grew right along with me.

In the blink of an eye, the town added a highway, shopping centers, a bowling alley, indoor skating rink, another elementary school, a middle school, a private school, and a police station. Then came three more bars, four more gas stations, fast-food places, a restaurant, a pizza place, two motels, a nightclub, and traffic!

The trees all died of Dutch elm disease leaving Mattydale looking as different as me in my military dress uniform, marching alongside my father in a town parade. He wore his American legion hat, on which his first division pin was prominently placed. My father marched with pride knowing I'd recently graduated from the Drill Sergeant's Academy at Fort Knox, Kentucky.

I had graduated from college before the academy but with very little fanfare. College was something my father could not fully comprehend. The army was something my father respected, understood, and was able to celebrate.

It was the kind of parade that every small town had with local officials riding in polished convertibles alongside smiling beauty queens. The high school band would be playing one of Sousa's tunes with an entire row of drummers supporting cheerleaders and majorettes twirling batons. They tossed the hypnotizing spinning extensions of their joy high into the air, catching them inches from the ground to the delight of the applauding crowd.

There were women's civic organizations whose members carried banners along with raffle tickets for homemade pies and other baked goods. Each kitchen in the neighborhood had been buzzing with activity for days as the local stores ran out of flour, sugar, and vanilla.

There were flags everywhere! The Boy Scouts waved them. The Girl Scouts waved them, and each fire truck and police car in the county had flags unfurled from every open window.

The sidewalks were crowded with spectators and children scurried along the parade route to catch the sweet hard candy being tossed by clowns with big red noses, polka-dotted oversize pants, and huge feet.

It was an outsized illusion that all was well in the world, even though World War II had dominated the headlines for years, the Korean War had just been wrapped up, and the Vietnam War was raging.

The parade I marched in prior to the one with my father was a completely different scene. It was an anti-war protest in Emporia, Kansas, during my college years. Everybody was singing "Kumbaya, My Lord," even if they had no religious belief and a lousy voice. There were no uniforms of note, but the young shaggy men had hair down to their collars or beyond. Lots of them were shirtless, wore bell-bottom pants, and walked barefoot. The young women wore very short skirts, tank tops without bras, and lots of beads. They handed out flyers that advertised the next rally and listed the names of every warmonger in Washington responsible for our country's participation in Vietnam. Any piece of candy that was handed out had a little bit of cannabis in it and was not for children but the child that was in every young adult. There were police cars and officers with clubs in case things got out of control. Nothing did! Hundreds of flags were flying that bore the image of a freshly silk-screened peace sign or doves as reminders of our purpose.

I was proud to be marching in that particular parade. I was convinced my generation was going to stop the war in Vietnam and maybe all wars forever!

My fellow marchers knew every word of Barry McGuire's song, "Eve of Destruction," and believed we were our country's best hope for peace.

Following the march in Emporia, there were speeches, poetry readings, a drum circle, and finally cold beers in the park where peace lovers swam in the nude and talked of free love. Condoms were out, the pill was in, and the planet was going to be saved!

It was the sixties and we believed there were more of us than them, them being the establishment. The harsh reality was that the establishment had the money, the power, and the connections. All we had were flowers in our hair and an idea. That wasn't enough!

We tried to change the world, but things in motion tend to stay in motion. The country was drifting toward supporting the military machine, big business, and new authority for a power-hungry president. The environment became a soft issue along with race relations and education as the government's stand on war hardened.

For fear the young and educated would delay or sideline the government's agenda, they instituted a draft lottery, resulting in the collapse of many war protests. The silencing of the majority of draft-age men, and the women who loved them, allowed the war to continue with full funding. War is expensive in many ways, but for some, war was a way of becoming millionaires. The Vietnam War prompted the massive spending of one trillion, in today's dollars. It radically increased profits for many politically well-connected companies.

In 1965, the evening TV news started to show American viewers some of what was happening in Vietnam, making it the first television war. By that time, our troops had already been there for five years, but nobody understood why we were there or what we were fighting for. We were told it was to stop the spread of communism, but that didn't happen.

This unwanted war became even more unpopular when graphic and upsetting images of the conflict were broadcast into homes during the dinner hour. This was horrifying to the draft-eligible young men who had been raised in part by Capt. Kangaroo and the Mickey Mouse Club.

There were protests, but the war continued, resulting in the death of over 58,200 Americans, two million civilians, as well as over one million North Vietnamese and Viet Cong fighters. Multiple thousands were injured!

The Vietnam War ended on April 30, 1975.

Who won? Nobody!

The parades kept marching.

Army Physical

I GOT MY LETTER FROM THE GOVERNMENT informing me of where and when I was to report for my army physical. My draft number was very low, so I was expecting the letter as well as fearing it. Despite the expectation, I read it over and over again, believing this couldn't be happening to me. I was close to college graduation and prayed I'd be able to get my degree before being drafted. Most deferments had been stopped, leaving jail and Canada the only options.

For me, there was no option but to comply. I felt as if I was betraying my generation, but I couldn't betray my father. I swallowed hard and collected my nerve for the ordeal.

A group of others who had received the same letter gathered outside our dorm, and we caught the bus to Kansas City. It was a very quiet ride. When we arrived at the induction center, we were led into the cafeteria where lunch was served. I couldn't eat but sat with two guys at one of the round tables, trying to keep my hands steady while sipping a cup of coffee. I had seen these other two on campus but did not know them. Not having a clue as to how they felt about the war and the draft or anything else, I kept my mouth shut until finally blurting out, "I hope I fail the physical." This opened the floodgates of anti-war rhetoric. Eventually they shared their names, numbers, and plan to fail the exam. Tom unfolded a small foil wrapper and showed me the pills they were going to take when their names were called.

"What are they?" I asked, not knowing if it was speed or acid or any number of substances available in a college town.

"What the fuck do you care?" Tom answered angrily. "It's an anti-Nam pill. It will keep you alive. The guy I bought them from said that two pills are all anybody needs. There's more than enough here for you if you want a couple."

"No thanks! What I do want is a restroom. Have you seen one?"

"It's just inside the lobby." Jim pointed. "Don't piss everything out. They might need some of that for their little white paper cup," he said as I walked away.

Once I got to the urinal, I was too nervous to pee. I stood there for at least two minutes before anything happened.

When I returned to the cafeteria, my tablemates were already on their feet, saying our names had been called. I downed the last of my coffee in one gulp and prepared myself for the unknown.

"Well, best of luck to all of us," I said, putting my cup back on the table.

"You'll be okay." Jim laughed. "I stirred two of those pills into your coffee."

"Oh, fuck," Tom interrupted with a look of terror on his face. "So did I!"

I didn't have time to react before we were whisked into different lines. I remember undressing, being weighed, having the doctor look down my throat, up my nose, and in my ears. Then there was the eye test, and I began to notice the letters were not staying still. My pulse was taken and heart listened to and finally came the mandatory bend-over-and-spread-'em test.

When I stood back up, I thought I was going to pass out. I couldn't seem to find my legs.

I kept on repeating to myself, "You can handle this. You can handle this! YOU CAN HANDLE THIS!"

I tried to, but it wasn't easy. I felt as if I had lost my sense of time and space. I was having great difficulty focusing and forced myself to hold onto reality by concentrating on the verticals and horizontals of each architectural element of the building I was lost in.

While being marched single file down a long narrow hallway to get dressed, I spotted Tom being marched, naked, in the opposite direction. As we passed, I reached across the divide and punched him in the jaw with all my strength, knocking him out cold. He fell face-first onto the tile floor. Several others tripped and fell on him. One of them was Jim.

I had great difficulty figuring out how to put my pants on, and tying my shoes was absolutely impossible. After numerous failed attempts, I decided a knot would have to do. I remember walking with some other young men to the bus station. I didn't even know my name or the whereabouts of the ticket I was asked for at the bus door. Luckily, a couple of guys who had been on the bus that morning vouched for me. They guaranteed the driver that I was another college student who had just finished the physical and needed to get back to Emporia. He let me on the bus.

Everything was a blurred dream of being upside down in the baggage section at the rear of the coach. Nothing made sense. Some strangers helped me off the bus in Emporia, and while stumbling past a local beer joint on Main Street, a student from my dorm took my arm and walked me up to the fourth floor and my room. I slept for two days.

I did see Tom and Jim the following week. Tom was missing two teeth, and Jim had a broken arm. We did not talk.

Later I found out they had both failed their exam. I had not!

I had been the one preaching anti-violence and thought I should feel guilty about their injuries, but I didn't. They tried to take away my right to choose for myself, and I couldn't tolerate that! I was in the middle of discovering who I was and wasn't about to accept a stranger making a decision for me. I was embracing my individuality and taking responsibility for my own actions, not anyone else's!

Punching somebody in the face was a bit out of character for me, so I blamed it on the drugs and let it go. I had punched and been punched before, but it was far from a regular behavior. Fighting was something I could do. I wasn't afraid of it or doubted my ability to stand my own ground. It just didn't mesh well with my personal philosophy or world view.

I was into logic and thoughtful compromise as well as the whole peace movement. That's why I marched, and that's what separated me from my father. He was a World War II hero, but that had been in a very different war. At least that is what he believed and what I had been taught.

The longer I was in college studying art, history, and philosophy, the more I began to see greed as the basis for all wars throughout all time. I didn't share that personal insight with my father. I never brought war into any of our face-to-face times because it always triggered his war stories. They had been the main topic of every conversation for as long as I could remember. When I was a kid, I wanted him to talk about my winning the science fair for three years in a row or building a crystal radio or even girls, a topic in which I had a growing interest. That wasn't to be. It was always war talk, or to be more accurate, it was a war monologue. Even on the rare occasions when my mother convinced him to take me on a road trip, it was to first division conventions where hundreds of veterans told their stories and I listened. I listened for as long as I could and then I pretended to listen while thinking there must be something else to talk about other than war. They didn't talk about their jobs, wives, children, hobbies, interests, or even the future. Occasionally there was a reference to football, but even that seemed to carry the same strategies and emotional impact as the war stories.

At one of the conventions, he introduced me to a man named John Patterson, who held my face and said, "Wow! A miniature Chuck Page! Exact same eyes! He's going to make a great little soldier!"

I wandered away from the storytellers and took the elevator back up to our room, hoping that being a soldier would not be in my future.

I was wrong! Passing the army physical during the last semester of my senior year of college put a lot of things into motion that were not part of my long range plan.

My knowing that the war might be just around the corner made each experience uniquely special. Every book I read, lecture I heard, and conversation I was a part of became increasingly more important. Even the littlest of things were magnified. I was experiencing everything as if it was the last sip of a cold beer on a hot day, and I wondered if I'd ever have another. For the first time, my own death was on my mind.

I had thought about the likelihood of my mother's death because it had been part of the family dynamic ever since the cancer diagnosis years ago. But despite the number of doctors who repeatedly predicted she'd have only six months to live, she kept living! This reinforced the possibility of death being something with which you could reach a compromise.

I had to rethink this when I saw videos of American soldiers being mowed down by enemy machine guns. It was immediate and so very permanent! This did not show time for any negotiations.

So at the moment when I was primed and ready for life, my own death became possible. I knew that death had been around for as long as life and found that cycle of events to be indisputable. I questioned the acceptance of war as part of that cycle and why humankind had not been able to rise above that disaster. In school, history had been taught according to dates of wars, instead of dates of great inventions, works of art, and acts of enlightenment. We were taught at an early age that this fiasco was as natural as needing to take the next breath.

I refused to believe that we couldn't do better, and I wanted to be a part of that effort. I didn't know how or when or where. All I knew was that I was committed to something that would make this world a better place, a place of peace where children could thrive, and education would flourish along with the arts and sciences. I wanted the truth to be the foundation of all endeavors and acts of kindness, compassion, and cooperation as the expectation, not the exception. I wanted to teach!

I didn't know at that point that I had a lot more to learn before I could stand in front of a classroom with confidence, but life took care of that!

Graduation

—

Worrying about final exams and term papers is challenging under the best of circumstances. Add to that stress the possibility of being drafted and concentrating on school became a personal battle. To make it worse, the peace movement was faltering. Only those who were being drafted showed up at the rallies. The rest didn't see the war as their problem anymore. They just looked the other way, forgetting the peace songs we'd sung and the bond we'd forged. I struggled with their shortsightedness and false friendship. Their newfound freedom from the possibility of Vietnam fractured the dorm and social gatherings. Even in the cafeteria, people sat according to their draft number.

Luckily, I did get to graduate! My parents and younger sister drove all the way to Kansas for the ceremony. My mother insisted the trip was going to happen despite health issues and the cost. I was thrilled they came. They got to see my name on the dean's honor roll and hear me announced as graduating with multiple honors.

It was difficult to leave college behind. I'd learned many things in the classrooms, the library, the dorms, and the local beer joint. Along with academic and social things, I also acquired some personal and emotional knowledge, like how hard it was to say goodbye to Terry. She was just completing her first year as an art major at the same college and lived in Pennsylvania. We had an immediate connection and promised to stay in touch.

All the goodbyes to fellow students, graduates, and professors were followed by the trip back to Syracuse to wait for my hello greeting from the draft board.

My sister and I drove the beat-up old car of mine home from Kansas. She was great company and listened to all my college stories, and I listened intently as she shared her high school adventures, including school plays and first real boyfriend. Though the drive was long, we were back in Syracuse all too soon, and I had to face the fact that another trip of a different kind would be required at any moment. It would be a trip with an unknown destination and no guaranteed return date.

I tried to get a decent summer job, but employers were not interested in anyone who might be called to report for military duty. The best I could do was to get a job mowing grass on the grounds of a steel mill and a drive-in theater. The steel mill was bad enough, but the drive-in was much worse. Used condoms kept getting bound up in the mower blades by those who realized the pill was not all the protection they needed. Going from being listed in the latest publication of Who's Who in America's colleges and universities to being expected to deal with the remains of somebody's sexual escapade pushed me completely over the edge. I quit but not before suggesting that condoms be sold at the drive-in's snack stand. They made big bucks selling those little pieces of latex!

I returned to Mr. Mike's Nightclub, where I wore a suit, had clean hands, and was welcomed back onto the dance floor. It felt good to be moving in random interpretations of the music instead of mindlessly pushing a noisy mower in straight lines. Mr. Mike's Nightclub had been my second home and where I worked part-time for years as a dance partner and escort to the ladies when their dates' attention was needed elsewhere. Mr. Mike had hired me when I was only fifteen. He'd been like a second father and mentor, opening my eyes to a very different world than what I'd been used to. My friend, Jake, was still tending bar; the ladies were still beautiful, and the money was good.

The highlight of my summer was when Terry came to visit. We got out our paints and sat in my parent's backyard with our canvases, talking for hours. She brought back all my college memories and dreams of teaching art and backpacking through Europe. Her visit grounded me and gave me a different focus. Instead of rushing to the mailbox every day to see if Uncle Sam had written, Terry and I took long walks or rode my motorcycle out by the lake. We pretended Vietnam was just something on the news and had nothing to do with me.

If only that had been true! The reality was that Vietnam was coming in a sealed envelope addressed to me and no amount of pretending was going to change that fact.

Being pressed into service was like being caught in a whirlpool. The water around the top edge flowed slowly, but as you rode the current to the center of the wet cyclone, everything moved faster. One minute you're wading and watching and wondering, and the next minute you're gasping for breath, trying not to drown.

Lots of my friends had already been drafted, deployed, and died. Some had survived the experience and picked up their life where they left it. Those lucky ones came back to their wives, girlfriends, jobs, college, and lifestyle without skipping a beat. Others came back missing arms and legs or pieces of their minds.

These were thoughts that floated in my head and mingled with the stories my father told of his time in World War II.

I was already feeling the pull of the current and was trying to keep my head above water.

The Plane

A MONTH AFTER TERRY'S VISIT, THE INEVITABLE happened, and I was on a military plane heading south. There was one stop in Washington to pick up more draftees, and then we were off to Louisiana. It was the first time I'd ever flown on a really big aircraft. I loved being so high in the air that I could see the curve of the earth. It reminded me of the world globe my mother had given me one Christmas. It was my favorite gift. I loved seeing the exact location of each country and their geographic relationship to each other. I'd taken the globe to college and hoped that someday I'd take it to my first apartment. There was no place for it where I was heading at that moment.

The flight made me wish I was going on a vacation and not on the way to basic training. I fanaticized my destination being Paris or Rome or one of the many places my art history teacher talked about. I closed my eyes and could almost hear her vivid descriptions of the ceiling of the Sistine Chapel and the gargoyles on Notre Dame.

I was shaken from my fantasies as turbulence buffeted the plane. We had flown into dark clouds and straight-line rain became all I could see out the window. We were beginning to descend when lightning struck, causing the engine I'd been staring at to burst into flames.

I remember all the lights in the cabin going out as the plane suddenly dropped hundreds of feet before recovering. My seat belt stretched tight across my lap, preventing me from hitting the ceiling, but those who were standing or in the lavatory were flung in all directions. Our meager meal was airborne and soda cans were ricocheting everywhere as luggage compartments spilled their contents and passengers puked.

After a deep dive and some steep swerves, the pilot got the plane under control enough for a wild side-skidding, bump-filled landing. We were pushed out of the plane and onto the wet tarmac in the middle of flames with sirens blaring, lights flashing, and confusion. From there we were herded onto a military bus as the injured were rushed away by ambulance. The storm had knocked out all the electricity on the airstrip and in surrounding buildings, leaving only the lights from multiple speeding vehicles and their distorted reflections to suggest a direction for our tentative steps. An army officer did a head count twice and asked if there were any others injured before ordering the driver to get us to the post as quickly as possible. The guy who had been sitting next to me got the officer's attention by saying his back was hurting and that he could hardly stand. When the officer went to get some assistance, that guy turned to me, smiled, and said this would keep him out of Nam! They took him away on a stretcher as our bus left the airport.

All I kept thinking as we drove through the rain was that the lightning had been a sign that I was not supposed to be there. Not only was that a sign, but as the bus drove onto the post, the chain across the road in front of the guardhouse had not been unhooked. Following another neck-snapping jolt, we busted through with emergency alarms ringing and soldiers running with flashlights to escort the new arrivals to Fort Polk.

I knew this wasn't where I should be, but I was, and I was determined to make my father proud. He had powerful recollections of his time in the army and the officers he served. He was proud of what they accomplished, the loyalty he felt for his comrades and his duties, which he called sacred. He loved our county and our flag, which he flew proudly every day. He never doubted the government's leaders and interpreted their decisions as the law. He was the product of his generation just as I am a product of mine.

I grew up during the age of the cold war, Sputnik, and the race to the moon, a time when everyone believed the United States was going to win by educating its youth. He was raised to take orders. I was raised to question them. He believed that loyalty came with the position. I believed that loyalty had to be earned. We both were raised to honor thy father! So there I was at Fort Polk, Louisiana, committed to sacrificing everything because I wanted my father's approval, respect, and love.

My father was a good man, and everybody loved him. He was handsome and kind with a servant's personality, willing to help anybody at any time. Like my mother, he left school following eighth grade. He was very good at math and capable of building anything. He had a natural mechanical ability and kept our old car running long after the guys at the local garage recommended it be towed to the junkyard.

Had my father been at Fort Polk, he would have been the first one reacting to orders, marching to the gate, repairing the chain, and rewiring the guardhouse. My father responded to an order without hesitation or question. It brought him to life and gave him purpose. An order enabled him to put his skills into action. It was taken seriously and obeyed. My father would never have considered any dereliction of duty. He believed in the chain of command, military honor, and that someone with authority had sanctioned the legal and moral aspect of any order.

I did not always understand my father's unwavering allegiance and blind obedience to a superior or a cause. I did, however, respect his authentic belief and determination to carry out what he saw as his duty.

Haircut

When the electricity was restored, we were marched to the showers, followed by a mandatory haircut and shave. I watched my hair fall to the floor in clumps that were immediately swept away. It wasn't like a regular barbershop. There were no mirrors to look into, prompting questions about liking the length of the hair. My appearance was the same as the guy next to me and the guy next to him and the guy next to him.

We were all given uniforms and underwear in the same shade of military green. Then we were gathered into a room and told that we were no longer individuals but army property! These words had significant impact on me, way beyond the haircut or uniform. The idea that I had gone from being a civilian with individual rights and the ability to have choices to becoming property was frightening.

The sergeant pointed to a wall lined with M-16 rifles, saying, "Look at these. Each one is exactly alike. Each one has the same purpose. None of them have a brain or any sense of self-determination. It is a thing to be used. It will be clean and ready for use at all times. Remember this! You are just another tool for the army to use! The army does not want or expect you to do anything other than what you have been ordered to do. Let me make this perfectly clear. I did not say asked to do but ordered to do! The army will give you a place to sleep, food to eat, exercise, training and comradeship. You will give the army obedience, loyalty, and attention. You are no longer in charge. The army is in charge. Your job is to do your duty! It is not to question! Your duty is in your orders.

"The army won't give you love. That was your mother's job. The army is not your mother! The army can only give promotions, and they come to those who are the best soldiers. The best soldiers carry out their orders in a timely fashion and then wait in silence, like the rifles on the wall. You are just a tool, like any other tool that the army has at their disposal. Tools don't think. They don't even think about thinking. You won't miss thinking. Thinking is overrated anyway! You will be busy. Being busy will occupy every moment. When you are not busy, you will be dead tired or just plain dead!"

I thought he was exaggerating, but I quickly learned that he was understating the army's ability to push the human body beyond anyone's expectations. Those who met each challenge were given greater responsibilities, and those who could not found themselves with a different set of orders.

I was designated to be a squad leader and later a platoon sergeant, where I was put in charge of sixty men. The progression went in this order: basic training followed by advanced infantry training, and finally The Drill Sergeant Academy at Fort Knox, Kentucky, for those few who made it that far. Many did not, including some whose greatest desire was to have those sergeant's stripes. It took more than size and strength to make the cut. You had to have endurance, restraint, resilience, brains, and balls! A lot of balls!

We were all required to endure the eye-burning, raw-throat, and choking effects of the gas chamber as we struggled to find and properly wear a gas mask in the dark gas-filled room. We had to know all the workings of multiple weapons, how to clean them and fire them. There were timed tests for each new device and opportunities to use them while crawling on our bellies in mud, under live fire!

To my surprise, I became a marksman, holding my breath, correctly sighting the target, and squeezing the trigger with great accuracy. Lots of things surprised me as my determination and strength grew with every passing day.

The weight of the helmet, uniform, armor, weapon, food, canteen, compass, first aid kit, and everything else a soldier carries adds up to about seventy pounds. Add to that the radio and other things needed in a combat zone and a soldier might be carrying 120 pounds. Now imagine marching with that load or doing double time. Double time is a command that requires a thirty-inch step at 180 steps per minute.

Once following a long stretch of double time through the swamps and up to a ridge, we stopped to eat our rations. Jones, one of the guys who had grown up in the concrete world of Chicago's inner city, said, "I don't think I can move another inch, much less the twenty-seven miles back to the base." Then he slipped off his pack and sweat-soaked fatigue top before leaning back against a tree.

At that very moment, a six-foot-long black snake fell from the tree, landing around his neck. He jumped to his feet, screaming like a caged monkey at the zoo, and ran around in circles while trying to shake off the scaly scarf. Eventually, he passed out and the snake slithered away. This was the only time I ever saw Sgt. Smith laugh. He was the one in command and had been so strict that we didn't think he was capable of laughing. We laughed, too, until we had to build a field stretcher and carry Jones back to the post.

It had been weeks since I'd laughed, and it felt good! It reminded me that I was a person and not just a number on a dog tag. That feeling didn't last long. All personal identity was scrubbed away like dirt in the steam and nakedness of the group showers.

In the end, we were just tools, like the sergeant said we'd be.

I saw a lot of big tough guys crumble and break under the demands and exhaustion of training. Each day included what seemed to be logicless orders delivered with dehumanizing, browbeating language, laced with profane and insulting commands. Each day another would-be drill sergeant washed out of the program. Each day I was more determined to get those stripes.

Mornings started at four! I don't remember when the day ended. I just remember standing in formation the next day and the next and the next. The nights were more like a coma than sleep. I didn't even dream!

I never got a letter from my father, but each mail call brought some news from home. My mother wrote about family stuff, the neighborhood, and what she was baking or canning. Sometimes she'd include clippings from the newspaper to keep me up-to-date on hometown happenings. I also heard regularly from Terry writing about the college life she was still experiencing. I didn't always read the letters on the day I received them. I'd wait until I thought I could handle the emotional whiplash!

I learned a lot about myself in the army. I learned I was tougher than I thought, and I learned about the power of a shared sense of duty. I also learned that I was more like my father than I ever imagined. There were times when I even felt him near me, perhaps closer than we'd ever been while living under the same roof. I always knew he loved me. I never questioned that, only why he kept a distance between us.

I didn't want to go to Vietnam, but I was trained and ready. I was just a few feet away from boarding that military transport when orders were changed, and suddenly I was given the opportunity to transfer from active duty to reserve status. I jumped at the chance and, within days, was back in Syracuse, New York, trying to remember what it was like to be in charge of my own life. It's not as easy as it sounds. It's amazing how quickly a person can get used to being told when to sleep, when to eat, and what to do. For some people, the need for those orders lasts for the rest of their life!

Having been fortunate enough to survive the training and escape orders for Nam, I transitioned back to civilian life with little difficulty, but a different challenge was yet to come. I didn't have a name for it at the time, but somehow it was familiar. I recognized it even though it wasn't completely what I'd witnessed before. It was disguised by exhibiting the exact opposite symptoms to the same illness.

I spent a year sharing an apartment with a friend who had just received his honorable discharge from the service. I had been stationed stateside, and he had been deployed to Vietnam, a fact he never let me forget! We had not seen each other for years and in that time lots had happened. The results of which increased the chance of our living together meaning dying together. I couldn't let that happen! I had already been exposed to trauma-related behaviors and knew that pain all too well.

My father gave me a detailed version of World War II in multiple stories that he repeated throughout my childhood. I often felt he knew those soldiers he talked about better than he knew me. I wanted him to know me, but it's hard to compete with memories and dead people.

My roommate, Danny, carried his war home with him, sharing it with me realistically as well as sadistically. Memories of fear, danger, anger, and internal conflicts tied him to duties he hated along with all those who gave him orders. Through his words and actions, Danny took me to the battlefields, back alleys, scorched earth, and blood-soaked mud of his ordeal. Not because he wanted to, but because that was what stayed in front of him twenty-four hours a day. They demanded to be present tense and forbid that which deserved its time in history from having its rightful place.

My personal version of Vietnam came through Danny. He was the conduit that connected me to the war. It exploded in front of me, jeopardizing everything, including my life, and so I left. I left and rarely looked back, even though his experiences stayed with me. I left carrying the sights and sounds of war along with guilt because I had not been able to help him. I tried, but his wounds were too deep and damaged too severely. I left in order to survive!

I never guessed the two of us would ever cross paths again in this very large world of ours. There are so many places to go, both above and below the equator. Between the latitudinal and longitudinal lines are billions of places to live and work and even hide.

I used to study the globe frequently! There are seven continents, 195 countries, over four million unique cities and towns, along with millions of roads for somebody to go anywhere they want.

No, I never expected to see Danny again, but it happened!

Syracuse Sidewalk

Danny and I hadn't seen each other for a long time, but I recognized him immediately when we passed on the street in Upstate New York that evening. He was much thinner, looked a bit worn, and had a lot of gray at his temples. Perhaps I noticed him because he still had his hair in the same military style. He hated that army buzz cut, but he always kept it that way as if it was an order he could not defy.

Every time I thought of him over the past many years, I thought of him as being dead. Danny was incredibly self-destructive and angry. I felt sure he had not survived. That didn't stop me from thinking about him, even when I didn't want to.

"Danny?" I called out without even thinking.

It was an automatic response, rooted in shock, more than a desire to make contact. I regretted it as soon as I said his name.

"Dave!" he responded while turning and slowly walking back toward me, cautiously extending his hand to grasp mine. "It isn't even Paris!" he said with a laugh, "but here we are on a sidewalk back in Syracuse, where it all began."

"That was a long time ago!"

"Quite a few turns around the sun, but here we both are! I thought you were living in Pennsylvania."

"I am. Terry and I have been here with the kids to visit with my folks over Easter break. We're on our way back now."

"Would that be the Terry I remember?"

"The very one!"

"Did you say kids?"

"Yup, three boys. They're right here in the car. The little one's asleep on Terry's lap. Come say hello before we head to PA. She'll be surprised to see you."

"I'll be there in a minute. I'm parked on the street, just a few cars behind yours. There's somebody I want you to meet."

I went to the curb and opened up the passenger door to tell Terry who I'd met. By that time, Danny was coming with a young woman, walking about three steps behind him. She was petite and pretty with short black hair and bangs cut straight just above her eyebrows. We gathered around the open door for introductions and greetings.

"Dave, Terry, this is Star," Danny said, giving me a slight smile while raising one eyebrow.

It was a quick encounter. I had to get on the highway before it got too late, and they were on their way to some bar with a name I could never pronounce as well as Danny was able to. He also referred to it as Little Vietnam. There was some information exchanged in the few minutes of small talk, but I don't remember any of it. My head was already spinning like the globe we used to keep in our old apartment. We said goodbye with no mention of ever getting together again, and they went back to his car.

As I buckled my seatbelt, there was a tapping on my driver's side window. It was Danny motioning for me to lower the window. I did.

Danny leaned in and spoke three words before quickly returning to his car. "I forgive you" were the words he spoke, and then he disappeared.

Terry had been attempting to feed our fussing baby and asked what Danny wanted.

"Just to say goodbye," I answered and then both cars were driving off in different directions.

In my rearview mirror, I watched Danny do a U-turn and merge into the city traffic. The kids all fell asleep quickly, which was the plan and so did Terry, which was not. It was just as well. I needed time to process the unexpected episode on the sidewalk. I needed to be alone with my thoughts in the falling darkness.

As the headlights turned on showing where I was going, memories illuminated my brain, shedding light on where I'd been. I had the next five hours to remember the past, and there was much to remember. It didn't all come back to me easily or in chronological order. It came back as if I was trying to remember a dream that I'd awakened from. It came in bits and pieces, out of order, and nearly forgotten. I figured I'd unpack it, like clothes that had been hastily thrown together for a quick exit. Everything needed to be straightened out and made sense of.

The unpacking started with the time Danny first told me he always called each of his girlfriends Star.

"Why Star?" I asked.

"I like that golden age of adventure comic strips."

"What comic strip in particular?"

"The best one! Don't you remember the banner? *Brenda Star Reporter*! She was a glamorous newspaper reporter who could figure out anything."

"If you have to call each girlfriend by the same name, why don't you call them Brenda?"

"Never! Star is much more special. There might be a million stars up in the night sky but not here on earth and not in my bed. I need one in my bed!"

Danny said this to me one hot September night while we were walking down North Broad Street in Lansdale, Pennsylvania. He'd been drinking after work again! When he returned to the apartment we shared, I suggested a walk to sober him up. Walking rarely did the trick, but at least it got him out of the apartment and moving. I had grown tired of sitting in the dark, listening to his drunken ramblings. Maybe taking a walk was more for me than Danny.

We were just passing a four-foot-tall spool of heavy-duty electric wire leaning against a telephone pole when he came to a complete stop. I thought he was going to throw up, but he pointed at the wire and spoke as if it was some kind of sign foretelling the future.

"This piece of industrial-grade cabling has been cluttering the sidewalk since we moved here. It's in the way! Nobody's using it or even knows what it is. It's just here, taking up space. It's fallen off the radar screen. Somebody has lost track of it. It's obviously got some worth. Its core is copper but nobody sees it. It's become practically nothing at all. Everybody's gotten used to it being there like dirt. Nobody has put it to work. Nobody has even stolen it. Nobody has unraveled it! Nobody gives a shit."

"So?"

"So I feel a kind of kinship to this piece of crap!"

"So now you have an emotional connection to this thing? I find that somewhat disturbing."

"You know what?"

"Doubtful but I'll bite. What?"

"I'm going to stay in this stinking town until the day it's gone. On that day, I'll be gone too."

"You're drunk!" I stated as we continued our walk.

"Of course I'm drunk. I'm always drunk or trying to get drunk."

"Why?"

"Why not?"

"Never mind! Let's not have that conversation again. Let's go back to the Brenda Star thing. As bizarre as it sounds, I understand that better than the drinking thing. Brenda Star was a redhead. Does that mean you only date redheads?"

"Not Brenda Star, just Star! Get it right!"

"Got it! Now about the red hair?"

"In my mind, they all have the same color hair once the lights are out."

"Tell me more about the name. I want to make sure I understand."

"I call each one Star. That way I never call any one of them by the wrong name," he said sincerely as if it made all the sense in the world.

"We better turn around. I've got to get some decent sleep before work tomorrow."

"You don't work, you teach!" Danny shot back. "If you want to find out what work is, come to the construction site with me tomorrow."

Danny didn't understand how hard I worked as a teacher and used every opportunity to discredit my chosen profession. He measured work by the number of calluses, pounds of sweat, and layers of dirt. He hated it when I called teaching work.

"I've told you a hundred times, David. Tell me you're going to school, not work. Work is my line!" Danny yelled out to the empty dark streets.

I didn't yell back. It wouldn't have been worth it, especially when he'd been drinking. I'd tried that before and it just got ugly. I kept walking. This Danny who I was walking with was not the Danny I'd known before the army. The Danny I'd known was quick with a smile and one of the smartest high school seniors I'd ever met. His older sister introduced us during my sophomore year at the community college. Liz and I were in the ski club together as well as biology class. Sometimes we'd meet in the student center for a snack in between classes.

We were there one day when Liz's friend, Rita, came in to warm up after walking six blocks in blizzard conditions from the center of Syracuse. The two of them had graduated from high school together six years earlier and were latecomers to the college scene, trying to retool their lives.

When Liz first introduced me to Rita, both Rita and I politely shook hands, cementing the appearance that we'd never seen each other before. In reality, I'd met her at Mr. Mike's, a club where my job was to keep the ladies occupied on the dance floor during the men's business meetings. The ladies' smoking lounge, restroom, and visiting guests at nearby tables were other distractions, but my services required a little cash from their escort.

"Is that man your husband?" I asked during my first waltz with Rita.

"He's somebody's husband," Rita answered and then asked, "Who taught you how to dance like this?"

"An old pro," I replied and then we just danced until I received a signal from the table, letting me know the meeting was over and my services were no longer needed.

"You should give lessons," she said as I dropped her off at the table.

"No, I need more practice with my pivot and turn. I bet you could teach me some interesting steps," I whispered.

I knew I was way out of bounds but took the gamble anyway. Her date was already on his feet, ready to take her hand. He pushed some bills into my pocket and then they walked to the center of the dance floor. Twice she looked back at me while they were dancing. I placed my right index finger to my lips and shook my head as if to say, "That joker can't dance at all!" She smiled!

The next thing I knew, Jake, the bartender and my friend, had his hand on my shoulder, directing me out the front door with determination.

"What the hell do you think you're doing?"

"What are you talking about?"

He smacked me hard on the side of my head and shouted, "Don't play the fool with me, asshole! You don't think I saw exactly where your hands were on that dame's hips?"

"We were dancing!" I shouted back.

"What? I wasn't born yesterday! I'm gay, remember? I can smell an erection from the lobby! That broad with the boobs was turning you on. Admit it!"

"Okay! You're right."

"That idiot she's with may not be able to waltz, but he could do a tap dance on your face that would leave a mark!"

"Sorry, Jake, I just lost my head for a minute."

"Make sure it was just for a minute! Now go wash your face in cold water and get out of here. I'll cover for you," he said while rubbing the side of my head where he smacked me. Then as I turned to walk away, he kicked me in the ass.

Rita and I met for the second time during our freshman English class at the community college. We had been seeing each other periodically but not at Mr. Mike's! She had promised herself to initiate a permanent course correction in her life, and that included going back to school, among other things. Rita only had three classes on Tuesdays and was coming straight from her job at an upscale jewelry shop on Salina Street when she entered the student center. She was shivering and covered with snow. It was April, but it was also Syracuse, and because of that fact, we all knew that winter might be around for another month or more.

"I can't stand any more of this weather!" Rita moaned while pulling off her coat, which shed frozen white crystals all over the floor.

I liked watching Rita pull off her heavy winter coat and shake the snow out of her long dark hair. She reminded me of a model Edward Degas might have used when he painted *After the Bath*. Voluptuous, to say the least!

"I wish we could get out of here for a while," Rita said with a sigh, pushing a chunk of ice onto the tile floor.

"Let's do it!" Liz blurted out. "Let's pool our funds and head south for spring break."

"What funds? I'm barely going to make tuition," I said with despair as Liz ran off to get Rita a cup of hot chocolate.

"Are you still working at Mr. Mike's?" Rita questioned, looking over her shoulder to make sure Liz wouldn't hear. Rita knew I always tried to keep the club separate from other parts of my world.

"I am but it's getting a little weird around there, and I'm thinking about—"

"Don't quit! Just take a little break," Rita insisted. "It will all look better after Florida."

I wanted Mr. Mike's to look better. I loved that nightclub. Over the years it became my home away from home, but the club had changed and so had I. As a teenager, I saw it all as a glamorous movie set where I played a minor character. There were low lights, good music, and a hint of danger. The lighting and music were still the same, but danger had taken a larger role in the changing plotline.

Liz came back, all excited, with an idea to make the trip more affordable.

"I know my kid brother would love to get off this iceberg for a while. He'd be thrilled to pitch in some bucks and come along."

"Is his dream to become a gym teacher too? I'm not sure I could spend that much time in a car with sports being the only topic," I teased.

"No, David, that's my dream. Danny only dreams of his girlfriend. Yuck!"

"My dream is getting to Florida," Rita said, slapping her hand palm down on the cafeteria table. "Who's with me?"

"I am!" Liz shouted, laying her hand on top of Rita's.

"Okay! I'll be part of this insanity," I said while completing the hand sandwich. "I don't know how I'll get out of work, but I do need a break!"

Liz jumped to her feet and started singing out, "We're going to Florida! We're going to Florida," while Rita whispered, "Tell Mr. Mike you really do need a break. You said he's good to you!"

I thought about that, but in the end, Jake, my favorite bartender at the club, said he'd take care of it for me. He told Mike I had to study for exams. Jake said he'd knock my block off if I came back looking too tan for the lie to be believed.

It was decided we'd take Liz's old Plymouth because it had a big trunk and was more reliable than my wheels. Her car was recently inspected and had a set of new tires. It wasn't anything to brag about, but it ran without leaving a trail of smoke and drips of oil.

I had used the nightclub I worked at as a possible excuse for not going to Florida, but that was only partially true. My mother had been fighting cancer for years, and I had it in my head that if I was there, I could keep the cancer at bay.

When I mentioned the possible trip to my mother, she responded with "I'll help you pack!"

My mother and I talked as we packed. She'd never been south of Baltimore but had heard of all the fantastic sights that could be visited and gave me twenty dollars for fresh oranges and grapefruits. I tried to give it back, but she wouldn't take it. The money came from an old coffee can she called the emergency fund. It was always kept on the top shelf of her closet. When I was a kid, it never held more than a couple of dollars in coins.

She seemed more excited about the trip than me and was sure that I needed a break from the books, the lectures, and the studying! No one in my entire family had graduated from college before, and she wanted me to be the first. My mother believed that a balanced life which included some fun would increase my chances of educational success. I agreed and kept packing.

For years, I had multiple part-time jobs to keep the household solvent. This had put a dent in childhood experiences, and my mother knew it. I think that is why she didn't hesitate to support the spring break. She wanted me to have it all, even though it was coming a bit late.

I wanted it all too but was used to accepting what I got and being grateful for it. I kept my focus on school, my two part-time jobs, and the dream of getting a four-year degree, as well as a position teaching art. I was completely aware that teaching was not going to make me rich, but it was going to make me happy, and I hung onto that dream. Lots of my friends were in college majoring in engineering, finance, or the medical profession. They'd give me a hard time about how I'd need additional side work for the rest of my life.

I'd generally respond by saying, "Let your future wife know I will be available for night work. Satisfaction guaranteed!"

Of course, this brought about a lot of laughter, but I did think seriously about the need for a decent income, and I had a plan. I was going to paint and sell my works in galleries and at street fairs. That was the plan, but I had no idea how difficult it would be to sell original work, especially as an unknown artist during rough financial times. I didn't want to be poor and promised myself I'd never let that happen. I wasn't afraid of hard work and liked to save. I was convinced I could make enough money somehow.

When I was in grade school, I received a small dime bank that was shaped like an old-fashioned cash register. It was a birthday present, and I loved it! The bank was designed to automatically open and ring once ten dollars' worth of dimes had been deposited. This motivated me to do all kinds of little jobs around the neighborhood, like collecting glass bottles for recycling, raking leaves, shoveling snow, and cleaning gutters. I had a growing excitement every time I'd press another dime into the slot and watch the mechanical display show the amount of my savings.

Unfortunately, I never got to see that bank or any others open up. There were always some financial needs in the family that required the bank to be broken into before it reached its limit.

I didn't care about the money. I would have gladly given that to my parents, but I wanted to see the little drawer open by itself and hear the bell ring.

The Trip South

There was a flurry of phone calls between Liz, Rita, and me over the next few days having to do with picking up a variety of snacks for the ride and agreeing that the topics of final exams and term papers were off limits. By Friday evening, in the midst of a major snowstorm, Liz and her brother pulled into my parents' driveway with Rita in the back seat.

Danny looked like a taller version of Liz with the same freckles. His hair was longer than hers and parted on the same side. They both were sandy blonds and had similar features, except Liz had blue eyes and Danny's were brown. He was not as flamboyant as Liz but then again nobody could be. She could find humor in a trip to the restroom and was very capable of sharing it hysterically, even if it wasn't especially funny. Danny was more reserved and philosophical by nature. He looked like someone who belonged on a cross-country track team, muscular and lean. He immediately joined in the conversation with astute observations and engaging insights. My fears of any awkwardness regarding age differences disappeared into the falling snow as we headed toward Route 81, avoiding the many cars that had slid off the road.

I had been nominated to be first at the wheel because of the icy roads. Liz said that since my father was a bus driver,

I probably had the best driver's training for the rough conditions. The plan was for Liz to drive next and then Rita followed by Danny. That was the plan, but I drove twenty-four hours straight to Florida. I didn't mind. Driving was and still is something I love to do. Maybe that is something I inherited from my father who never tired of being behind the wheel.

Along with excited conversations and a bit of nonsense, we played stupid road-trip games for hours. I wasn't sure Rita would be into this foolishness, but even if it wasn't her thing, she never let it show. It's possible that Rita needed to discover the kid in her as much as I needed to discover that in myself. Danny made up the rules and was very good at it. We were supposed to search for every road sign and try to be the first one to read it out loud. This had to be immediately followed by three words each starting with the same letter the sign started with. Those additional words had to be related to the Florida trip.

My worries that Rita might not buy into the spirit of the moment faded quickly. Despite the fact that she'd been out in the grown-up world for a while, she played along. This was definitely kid's stuff, and to my surprise, she joined in with giddiness. Maybe she needed this more than I did, and perhaps she wasn't quite ready to be as grown-up as she acted. I found seeing her being completely silly to be kind of beautiful!

"Song Mountain!" Liz shouted followed by, "Shells, sharks, and seagulls!"

Liz also added the rule that if you didn't respond quickly, any person that went before you get to punch you in the arm. Liz was a very physical person!

"Courtland!" Rita yelled. "Coastline, crocodile, and Clearwater."

"Binghamton!" Danny called out while pointing at the snow-drifted sign. "Beaches, bathers, and boats!"

"It's up to you, David," Liz threatened. "I've already folded my hand into a fist!"

"Susquehanna!" I screamed at the last possible minute. "Sunrise, sunset, and sunburn!"

Liz wanted to disqualify my entry because each of my three follow-up words all started with sun, but Danny was able to override Liz's complaint because he made up most of the rules.

The longer we played, the more stupid the words became. When Liz yelled "Delaware!" and followed it with "Dickhead, douchebag, and duck shit," Danny and Liz laughed their asses off.

Rita said in a very serious tone, "I know a guy that fits that same exact description."

The others laughed, but Rita wasn't trying to be funny. I wondered if it was that guy who couldn't dance.

We played the game all the way to the next state border, but the rules had begun to change drastically. At this point, there only had to be two follow-up words but both required a sexual connotation. When Liz yelled, "Maryland," followed by, "Motherfucking, masturbator," I almost drove off the road.

Eventually, Liz and Rita ended up sleeping in the back seat while Danny stayed wide awake with me in the front talking all the way. I was happy to have his company. The snow was still falling, and it was great to have another set of eyes on the road. Since we were total strangers and I had no preconceptions, we started with a clean slate. Nothing was really off limits, and we had the entire night in front of us.

My head had been in the books for months as I tried to keep my grades in a place that would keep me eligible for a scholarship. The spring break started by giving me the chance to talk, and I realized I hadn't done too much of that for quite a while. My job at Mr. Mike's included conversations, but they were within a very limited range of topics bordered by strict time frames and intentions. Behind the wheel of Liz's car, I felt free to go anywhere and say anything.

I loved the sense of freedom that came with the open road. Even though we had a particular destination and a map, the feeling of being in motion thrilled me. My butt had been glued to a chair in the library for months, and the longer we drove through the porous wall of snow, the more I knew that I made the right decision regarding taking this trip.

Danny was particularly interested in the map, which he studied meticulously while making sure I never missed a turn. Every time I asked him how far it was to the next big city or state-line he'd go to work using the map's key to give me an exact answer. Danny would also tell me the name of rivers we were crossing, roads we were running parallel to, and where we might find the next restroom or cup of coffee. He would have had his nose stuck in the map all the way to Daytona Beach if I hadn't made him talk about other things.

"So, Danny, I hear you're graduating in a couple of months? What's your plan after high school? College?" I guessed.

"I have a plan, but it's definitely not college, at least not right away. I'm going to join the army. I'm not going to wait around to be drafted. I've got good grades! I'm fit and healthy. I've got perfect vision too. I know I can ace the ability test and get a cushy job. I'd love to get into some kind of special duty, like code breaking. I'll put my time in the service and then let Uncle Sam pay for my college education."

"Do you have any reservations about what's going on in the jungle over there, on the other side of the world?"

"No! I don't think it will last. There are still protests, and the big shots in Washington want to keep their jobs. Voters don't like the sound of war! I'll bet the entire Vietnam thing will be over before I get out of boot camp. I'll never be deployed!"

"I hope you're right, but sometimes politicians play with words. A recession becomes an economic downturn, a race riot becomes a minor disagreement, and a war becomes a police action or conflict."

"Even if it gets to be a mess, I'll have a desk job someplace far away from the action. I've already met with an army recruiter three times, and he doesn't see a problem with my signing up."

I disagreed with Danny's perspective but decided to change the topic. It was his dream, and I didn't want to mess with it. We had just met. He was young, and this was our vacation. It wasn't the right time or place to get into a debate.

"Got a girl you'll be leaving behind?"

"Yup! Boy is she pissed that I'm taking this trip. I told her it will be a good trial run for when I leave for the service."

"Is she in your high school class?"

"No. She's only a junior. That's why her parents would never have let her join in this adventure."

"Did you ask?"

"No. Liz said Joann was too young and that the car would be too crowded."

"Is this a serious relationship, or are you just dating?"

"We're going to get married as soon as she graduates!"

"Wow! Marriage, that's a big step. What's she like?"

"She's great! She's beautiful and she'll wait for me."

Danny was in love as much as any eighteen-year-old could be and just as naive. He went on and on about Joann, how they met, what music they listened to, and where they liked to hang out. I enjoyed listening to his innocence. In fact, I might have been a little jealous. I had lost that long ago. Maybe I never even had it. Danny talked about how the two of them would spend hours on the phone every night, laughing and making plans for their future. He believed it was all going to happen, and I wanted it to happen for him even though I suspected there might be some sharp turns on that highway to happiness.

Danny only saw the road ahead filled with great opportunities, love, peace, and joy. I had no intention of bursting that bubble. The more he shared, the more I wanted Danny's dream for the entire world!

He talked a little bit about his mother and how she wasn't into the idea of his signing up for service. He thought she was just trying to baby him, and he didn't like that. He said he never mentioned the marriage thing to her for fear of a major battle. Danny said he loved his mother and that she had always been a positive influence and support while he was a kid. Now he wanted her to stay out of his business and give him a little space.

He asked me if I understood his need for greater independence, and I took that opportunity to get him thinking about the bigger picture.

"Sure, I understand! We all get to a point where independence becomes our goal. It's natural. Just make sure you don't mistakenly jump from one controlling situation to another, thinking that it's freedom. At least your mother's concerns are based on her love for you."

"I hear what you're saying, but I've got a plan that will work. My mother doesn't want to hear about my plans. She just wants me to be a kid and stay at home. That isn't going to work for me! What kind of a home did you grow up in?"

"I had a remarkably loving and solid family. There wasn't much money, but my sisters and I learned to deal with that. Unfortunately, cancer found a way to slither into our home. That was more difficult to handle. It was a constant source of worry but didn't put a stranglehold on anything. A foundation of hope had been built to smooth out the bumps in the road."

"Who has cancer?"

"My mother! She believes there is a lesson in everything, including the lack of money and the cancer. My mother always says that living from paycheck to paycheck will pay off big in building financial resilience and that we should be grateful. I worked all kinds of part-time jobs and learned a hell of a lot that wasn't part of any curriculum taught in school. My mother's way of dealing with cancer is a deeper lesson in resilience that guides me every day of my life. She says, 'So it's cancer. Let's go out for ice cream!'"

"How about your father?"

"Kind, gentle, generous, and loving! We don't spend too much time together. He works a lot."

"My dad died before I was born. I always wanted a dad to hang out with."

"Me too!"

"I'm going to be a dad someday. Joann and I want to have two kids. I can't wait."

"You're chasing after that grown-up world. There's no rush. Take some time!"

I decided I might have said too much and let that topic drop, but my childhood stayed in my thoughts. The circumstances of my household required me to grow up fast and make decisions I might not have been ready for, but I have no complaints. Life is what it is and then you have the chance to make it what you want. Maybe that's why I was attracted to Rita. She was beginning to make changes in her life, and I was impressed with her determination. Perhaps the same was true for Liz, but she never talked about her past and seemed to live very much in the moment. All I knew was that she'd discovered working at the insurance office was not for her and so she registered for college. She loved being where the action was, sports and lots of laughter. Liz decided she wanted to be around people who shared the same interests and set her sights on being a high school phys ed teacher.

Life had pulled one big punch on Danny before he was born, when his father died. Though he never felt the direct impact of that loss, he lived with the ramifications. His mother eventually remarried, and life went on. Nothing earth-shattering had ever rattled or changed his world. His mother doted on him from day one. Liz had always been like a second mother, and she was determined to protect him from everything, including girls like Joann.

I had learned long ago that no one can be protected from change because that is exactly what life is. I also learned that change comes in many disguises. It may look like a guy who can't dance, college, an army recruiter, or even Joann.

It's amazing how much can be shared in a small space only being lit by the amber glow of the dashboard. Danny and I tossed topics back and forth for hours without a bit of silence. Conversation was fun and easy, and suddenly the sun was rising.

Liz and Rita sat up and we rolled down the windows, letting the sea air blow all our yesterdays away. I didn't think about school or money or Mr. Mike's. For that moment, there was no war, no cancer, and no clouds. Everything was new and exciting and available!

I put my left arm out into the welcomed heat and let the party begin. With my sunglasses on and radio blasting out the Beatles' pop hit, "Hey Jude," I sang along as if I was in the band and on a world tour. Within minutes, we were all singing, and to my ears, the harmonies were perfection.

The land was very flat, and there were palm-tree shaded freshwater lagoons everywhere. None of them were covered in ice, and this made me very happy. It all looked like a very different world, and that was exactly what I needed.

I had always wanted to travel, and this was my first big trip. Absolutely nothing looked anything like what I was familiar with—not the trees or the flowers, not the street signs or styles of houses. The rooflines of the houses in Syracuse were steep, so the weight of heavy winter snows would be transferred to substantial vertical beams along the perimeter of the house. Many of the houses in Florida had flat roofs or ones with very little slant at all. Florida houses had carports instead of garages, and there seemed to be a pool in every backyard. I had never seen so many convertibles in my entire life, and all the cars seemed to be rust free and clean.

Because everything looked different, I felt different, and that made me want to travel even more and discover how I would feel all over the world. I shared that thought over the phone to my mother when I called from a rest stop to let her know we'd arrived in Florida.

She said, "The world will come to those who don't get the chance to get out into it. You can feel differences in your own backyard if you let them in."

I knew that was true, but I was still very happy to be someplace different.

Daytona Beach

When we arrived in Daytona Beach, I was energized by the cloudless sky and first glimpse of the ocean. I knew that it was only a matter of minutes before exhaustion would demand my attention, so I began looking for a cheap motel that had a vacancy sign.

An hour passed as we drove up and down the strip, looking for what seemed to be the impossible. There were tons of ice cream shops, beer joints, and restaurants with huge signs advertising fresh seafood. Everywhere I looked, I saw fancy hotels that had pools, hot tubs, air-conditioning, and bars. There were places to rent surfboards, bicycles, motor scooters, scuba-diving equipment, and boats, but we saw nothing about a cheap room.

When I spotted a traffic cop sliding a ticket under the windshield wiper of a new Corvette Stingray, I pulled over and explained our dilemma.

"You're on the wrong street, kid," he said with a huge Irish smile. "This here is the main drag. It takes big bucks to bed down in this neighborhood! Take a look at the cars parked on this street, Lamborghinis, Mustangs, Barracudas, and Corvettes. Does your car look like it belongs here?"

"Not by a long shot!"

"Go up to the next light and turn right. Continue three streets back from the coast and take a left. Look for Max's Motel on the right-hand side. Tell him Sean sent you!"

"Thank you for the information. Anything else I should know?"

"Yup! Don't get high. Don't get drunk. Don't get in any fights and don't get anybody pregnant!"

"Is there anything I should get?"

"Yes! Get some sleep! You look terrible!"

Ten minutes later, we were hauling all our crap into a couple of adjoined rooms at Max's.

The motel was nestled in between a place that sold cotton candy and an arcade, whose pinball machines would be knocking and pinging all night long. There was a pool, but it was empty except for some dried palm leaves and a few inches of scummy green water. None of that mattered. There were four single beds, and I was in one before the others finished carrying in their stuff.

I thought I'd fall instantly to sleep, but I kept seeing the road coming up in front of me. I thought about my father and wondered how he managed to drive the same streets for so many years, waiting for someone to pull the signal chord, ordering a stop.

Eventually, I woke and found a note saying where I could find the group on the beach. I got into my bathing suit and headed to the water. The note said to look for one of the bright-red bedspreads that they were taking off one of the beds in the room the girls were sharing. By the time I found them, they were as red as the thing they were laying on. I woke them, so they could roll over or go back to the room. It was already way too late for suntan lotion!

I splashed into the surf. It felt cold, tasted salty, and woke me up to the reality that we were on spring break. I had seen pictures of college kids on spring break in Florida but never had pictured me as being one of them. I'd even seen movies and newsreels of this happening but always thought it was for some rich kids who went to Ivy League colleges and were always on the dean's list without having to try!

Blocks away from Liz's old Plymouth and Max's Motel, I was just another one of the party makers shoulder deep in blue waves and feeling like I was in the movies. Soon, the others joined me in a raucous water-bound wrestling match that transformed us into ten-year-olds. Then with Liz on Danny's shoulders and Rita on mine, each team tried to knock the other team down. I'm still surprised that no one drowned.

At around six o'clock, we dragged our tender bodies back to the room to shower and change. We could not afford any of the fancy seafood restaurants but found a pizza place called Pat's Fat Ass Pizza. Liz loved the name and insisted we had to eat there. Pat, who was really the size of a pretzel stick, prided herself in making all kinds of unique pizzas. They included toppings ranging from pineapples and chocolate chips to avocados, fresh lettuce, and walnuts. Her daily special was a plain pizza topped with macaroni and cheese.

Ordering took forever! There were too many choices, and Liz became totally distracted by the multiple big TV sets that hung on the walls showing sporting events of every kind. Finally we decided on an entrée called Pats' Seafood Taste-of-Heaven pizza, which amounted to a regular plain pizza with canned tuna fish spread all over. It was actually pretty good, or I might have been starving!

Every day we divided our time between the beaches and sightseeing. We could only afford one meal a day, and it was always at Pat's Fat Ass Pizza. Pat thought we were a hoot and really hit it off with Liz. Sometimes Pat used two cans of tuna because she thought we needed more protein. We always left a tip, and Pat always refused it.

I really did feel like I was living a dream. I had never been this far south before, and to be baking in the sun while knowing Syracuse was still under three feet of snow was fantastic.

We did not waste a moment! We saw the Kennedy Space Center, Everglades National Park, Sea World, Manatee Springs, Cypress Gardens, and a drive-by of Disney World!

At the end of the week, we piled all our belongings into the Plymouth along with a bag of shells, a crate of citrus fruit, and an entire large pizza for the road. The pizza was a gift from our friend, Pat, who gave Liz her contact information and a hug. We slowly joined the caravan of cars, sporting northern license plates, leaving the sunshine state and feeling a little blue.

None of us were ready to go but term papers and final exams were pulling three of us back. Danny was being pulled back by dreams of Joann. He said he'd like to see her in one of those two-piece bathing suits.

Liz punched him in the arm and yelled, "Get a grip! She only wants you for your money."

"I think you should get your jaw wired shut," Danny insisted. "Everybody knows she wants me for my body," he said while holding up his right arm and flexing his bicep.

"That's not a muscle, that's a pimple!" Liz shouted.

The two of them teased each other and laughed until Rita intervened, letting me know that she'd had just about enough of the kid stuff.

I didn't say anything, but I agreed with Rita who expressed herself perfectly. "I want both of you to have your jaws wired shut. Now shut up so I can sleep!"

Danny said he'd behave if he could sit in the front with me. So after a quick stop for what Liz called a Chinese fire drill, we headed home. It was time. We were just about out of money, and I could not eat another slice of tuna fish pizza. After about four hours, the pizza which had continued to bake in the sun-filled rear window stank so much we had to dump it! I had been smelling something foul for a while but thought that someone in the group had a personal problem.

During the dumping process, Danny leaned over to me and whispered, "I knew I'd get the front seat if I got a little rowdy. Now we can talk all the way home."

We did some talking and I was glad. His company and laughter seemed to extend the vacation.

Traveling North felt like we were going backward in seasons, from summer to winter. At first we had the windows opened all the way then partway then closed shut. It was inevitable but still a shock to the system when we had to turn on the heat as we reentered the white world of drifting snow. Each stop for gas, a restroom, or hamburger required a change of wardrobe. We went from shorts and a T-shirt to long pants and sweaters and eventually boots and winter coats.

When we were heading south, the car was filled with excited talk in anticipation of our adventure. Now the mood was more somber as we faced the realities associated with school and work and other responsibilities.

Danny and I did talk, but it was different. On our way south, each sentence seemed to overlap the previous one. Now there were long periods of silence when Danny slept, leaving me alone with my thoughts—worries about my mother and leaving my job at Mr. Mike's. I loved working at the club. I had been hired because I knew how to dance, and I knew how to dance because my mother had taught me.

My mother and father had met at a dance and had married because of that dance. I was in this world because of that dance, and now my world was getting larger. I had done a lot of growing up at Mr. Mike's and was feeling that the dance steps at the club were only taking me in the same old circles like my father's bus route. The more I thought about it, the more sure I was that a decision had been made. All that was left to do was to tell Mike, and that would not be easy. He could be a tough character and only liked the changes that he had ordered.

It's possible that spring break and the kid-like experience that it inspired had been what I needed to make the decision. Mr. Mike's, along with many other things, required me to act older than my age. I was tired of acting beyond my years. I wanted to embrace my own generation and live in my own time.

My thoughts bounced back and forth between the beach and the nightclub. The beach had given me a week of youthful exuberance. The nightclub had given me years of practice being an adult. I remembered how each holiday brought new decorations and new menu changes to fit the occasion. That memory reinforced my decision to leave. I had changed like the seasons and needed an updated menu to choose from.

Many silent hours passed in thoughts and memories as I pushed northward. I was forced to refocus on the road when Danny woke and announced his urgent need for a men's room. Of course, this meant tying this necessary stop to getting gas, purchasing snacks, and preparing for the last hundred miles.

We all zipped up our coats, wrapped scarves around our necks, and pulled on gloves as we readied ourselves to take care of all the immediate needs.

Danny, who was in severe bladder distress, hopped out of the car and began his mad dash for a urinal. Unfortunately in his haste, he forgot we were in the land of ice and not sand! He slid about ten feet with his arms outstretched as he made three complete slow-motion spins while battling gravity. During a move that looked somewhat like a Russian folk dance, he completely lost his balance along with the contents of his bladder. Finally while performing a series of insane acrobatics with accompanying sound effects and curse words, Danny landed on his back and slid into the snow-covered curb. Of course, the entire circus act was hysterical! Everyone was howling except Danny! When we pulled him to his feet, he immediately headed back to the car.

"What about the restroom?" Liz questioned.

"Too late," Danny responded. "I've got to get some dry clothes before my dick freezes to my pants."

This was the last big laugh of our trip, and we all regaled the event over and over, adding our own perspectives until we were in Syracuse.

Danny didn't mind our laughing at him. In fact, he laughed at himself and added personal details regarding the warmth of the piss as it reached his boots.

This was the prewar Danny. This was the kid I met for an impromptu spring vacation and a dose of sunshine. He loved to talk, share his dreams, and even laugh. He was fun loving, optimistic, adventurous, and a joy to be with.

Post Trip

I looked forward to seeing Danny again and finding out how his dreams were unfolding. I wanted to connect with every one of the spring break gang and foolishly thought this would happen naturally and often. It did not!

I always found it difficult to lose a friend and tried not to let that happen. Real friends are hard to find, and I cherished those who I'd bonded with. Lots of people acknowledge a fading friendship by casually saying, "We drifted apart." I never understood that! I always found the loss of a friend to be painful.

In reality, we were all in the midst of change and getting together became much more difficult than I had imagined. Time seemed to be moving faster and day-to-day circumstances prevented casual gatherings until seeing each other was only prompted by special events.

The four of us did meet following our trip so we could exchange photographs. The picture sharing resulted in the telling of stories about Pat's Fat Ass Pizzas and recalling the snowy night Liz farted in the car, and we had to put down all the windows for twenty minutes. We all laughed at the memory, but it wasn't as funny as living it. Somehow, even the photographs seemed to be of other people.

One time, we all met to celebrate Liz being accepted to a New York state college offering physical education, health, and biology majors. We also gathered together when I got a scholarship to the College of Emporia in Kansas to study art and education. I went to Danny's high school graduation with Liz and her mother. Liz's mother cried throughout the ceremony. Liz ignored what was happening at the podium, pointing out Joann, and saying the most derogatory things.

I stayed in regular communication with Liz, and I dated Rita for a while, which Liz didn't exactly handle well. Liz didn't like anybody seeing each other outside of the group setting. Liz had a childlike perspective, which was as joyful as it was unrealistic. Rita and I found ourselves able to have deep discussions on politics, philosophy, and life when Liz wasn't in the picture to interject a silliness that derailed adult conversations and behaviors.

Rita had her youthful side as well, but it was more age appropriate. Rita drove a motorcycle and was thrilled that I had recently bought one of my own. Hers was black and mine was blue. We called ourselves the bruised duo. The two of us were always finding some new stretch of road to investigate. Roads that took us way too far. It was fun as long as we were in motion, but once we were off the road, we both realized something else was happening. We never spoke about it. She knew I was going off to college in Kansas, and I knew she was six years my senior. It wasn't going to work and ended quietly. It didn't require words.

In time, I started seeing a girl I knew from high school. We had fun but nothing serious. We went to the movies, some parties, and a few picnics, but my mind was focusing on Kansas.

Soon, I was in the car for another long road trip as I drove to the Midwest, hoping I would find more of my youth that had been stolen by needing to be an adult too soon. I also hoped I'd find someone who would appreciate what Rita had taught me, someone I could share new adventures with.

Liz and I remained friends and exchanged letters while we were both finishing up our degrees in different areas of the country. She gave me updates on Pat and said she heard from Danny about every other week. He was in basic training in New Jersey and told Liz that it was a "cakewalk."

Once, the four of us had a single focus, a spring break fantasy! We crammed into a car for a twenty-four-hour drive to Daytona Beach, where we ate too much pizza, got too much sun, and swam with the manatees.

Now without a vehicle or goal to share, we were in separate parts of the country facing real-life situations and experiencing things that none of us could have imagined. Time was passing quickly, like the miles used to fly by. Perhaps moving forward in time is just like moving in space—they both take you to a different kind of place.

Rita stayed in Syracuse, met an older guy, fell in love, and got married. None of us were invited to the ceremony.

I finished my four-year degree and then, thanks to the military draft lottery, became a drill sergeant at Fort Knox, Kentucky.

In the middle of Liz's junior year, she attempted suicide and was hospitalized somewhere outside of Watertown, New York. I didn't find out about that situation until she'd already been released.

Danny was in Vietnam!

None of us heard from Rita again. My guess is that she blended into the adult world of children and mortgages, but I never knew for sure. I always pictured her as finding real happiness in that new world and understood why she needed to leave us behind. I don't think she ever forgot any of us. We were just the kids that she had grown beyond.

Liz stopped writing, but we did see each other the summer I got home from the army. I never asked her about the suicide attempt, and she never explained. She did go back to finish her degree and received a job offer teaching physical education in a small rural community about an hour outside of Syracuse. She begged me to apply for a job teaching art in the same district, but it just wasn't far enough away. And I needed some adventure in my life.

Liz told me that her brother, Danny, had completed his tour of duty and would be back in town the following week. Liz couldn't be there for his homecoming because of needing to attend a new teacher orientation and suggested I give him a call.

Following my discharge from active duty, I didn't know exactly what I wanted or where I wanted to go. I felt a little bit at a loss. I even drove out to Chicago to see if there was anything to pursue regarding that girl I'd dated from high school. She had moved there to take a job with the FAA. It took two minutes after my thirteen-hour drive to realize it was a wasted trip. I had been preparing myself for Vietnam for so long that this sudden civilian reality was somewhat hard to grasp. Every single thing I'd dreamed about regarding coming home became exactly what I wanted to run from. I feared staying in Syracuse would be too comfortable and prevent me from taking on challenges that would make me grow. I didn't want to be who I had been. I wanted more!

It was a time of some confusion. After being in a very orderly and structured environment where someone else was always in charge, I had to find my footing. In the army, there were instructions and timetables for everything. Out of uniform, I was suddenly my own boss. Even though I was happy to have it that way, it took some getting used to. I had to remember my old goals and dreams.

As a last-minute reach for something familiar, I called Danny, and we made plans to take a trip to Virginia Beach. I had promised my father I'd march with him in the annual town parade on that coming Saturday, so Danny and I decided to leave on Monday afternoon. All those years later, the two of us were going to jump in the car and head to another beach. It seemed like a good idea. We were strangers the first time. I had no idea we would be strangers again.

Change can go unnoticed when people see each other every day. It's a different story when years have passed, especially when those years were crowded with an avalanche of different experiences.

I thought about people from my past often but could only guess what their current lives were like.

I pictured Rita living in suburbia with her husband and a couple of kids. I thought she still had the motorcycle in their garage, under a tarp with an out-of-date registration. I don't think she'd ever get rid of it. Like a statue in the town square, it marked an important time in her history.

I imagined Liz having found the tools needed to keep her emotionally healthy and still possessing a Peter Pan perspective with lots of humor. I pictured her as ready to embrace her new job and anxious to inspire award-winning sports teams.

Danny was a complete mystery. I couldn't imagine him as a veteran of a foreign war. I only knew him as a kid, and that is how he had stayed in my mind. Other than a few updates from Liz, I only had memories of Danny and his dreams of Joann, long car rides, sunburns, sightseeing, tuna pizzas, and pissing his pants in a snowstorm.

I saw myself searching for a new beginning and wondered where and what it might be. I tried to see my future filled with purpose, travel, and a special person to share it with.

These were good imaginings laced with warm thoughts and memories that made me smile. I needed those recollections and looked forward to a time of catching up on the years that had passed since they were locked into place.

Even though the others were not going to be a part of this reunion with Danny, I was excited to hear their names being spoken. I also was ready to have some new experiences. I wanted to build memories that someday I could look back upon the way I remembered spring break.

I thought it would be like making deposits in an emotional bank account; I could periodically take withdrawals from if I needed a smile, a laugh, or a friend. Instead, it ended up being more like my childhood bank that was broken into and left empty.

Sometimes it's dangerous to imagine the future when having very little or no facts to guide your line of thinking. It's like the connect-the-dots activity elementary teachers used to give their students. The kids would use a pencil to sequentially draw a line connecting each numbered dot until a certain picture appeared. This time, there were too many missing dots and creating my own dots resulted in wishful thinking and a picture that was far from accurate.

When I was a kid, I used wishful thinking to deal with my mother's cancer. I shared that with her once, and she said that kind of thinking was a prayer. She said that prayers were the first step in building a road to where you want to be. I liked what she had to say and incorporated the behavior into my daily routine. The prayers didn't always get me to the destination I'd anticipated, but the trip was always an adventure.

My mother was no fool. She understood reality completely, but she also understood the power of the imagination. My mother believed there were times when imagining something pleasing helped put some sunshine into a dark stretch of facts.

I was about to see if that was true.

A Different Kind of Road Trip

I PULLED INTO THE DRIVEWAY AT DANNY's mother's old place and lightly tapped the horn just like I always used to do before getting out of the car.

Danny pushed open the screen door, tossing his duffel bag onto the porch while yelling back into the house, "Just shut the fuck up! I don't know when I'll be back or if I'll be back!"

He returned to the house for a minute and came out with a cooler of cold beer on his shoulder, letting the screen door bang shut behind him.

"Anything wrong?" I asked as I stood next to my car.

"No! Of course not! What could possibly be wrong on this perfect day in this perfect world? I was just giving my dear mother a kiss goodbye."

"So I heard. Very sweet," I said, matching his sarcasm.

"Leave this piece of shit of yours right where it is," Danny instructed as if he outranked me.

He walked by without even a hello, pulling open the garage door, revealing a brand-new Z28 Camaro, one of the hottest cars on the road!

"I just bought this chick magnet as a coming-home gift for myself! This thing will get us laid!" He laughed while shoving his bag into the trunk and tossing me the keys. "You drive. You always did. No reason to change what works."

"What about the beer? There's lots of room in the trunk. My stuff won't take up much space."

"Beer in the trunk? No! The beer goes in the back seat where I can reach it!"

I put my suitcase in the trunk and sat down in the leather bucket seat of this 255 horsepower sex machine and backed out of the garage. The low rumble of its eight cylinders echoed through a neighborhood that had only known rusting station wagons.

Danny reached for his first "beer for the road," as he called it, and laughed a laugh I didn't recognize. He lit a cigarette, blowing the smoke out his open window toward where his mother was standing on the porch. Danny gave her the finger and looked away.

I wanted to stop the car, cancel the trip, and leave. I couldn't come to grips with the fact this beer-swilling angry guy in the seat next to me was ever a friend of mine. I wanted to stop, but I didn't. I didn't even know why I continued with the plan. Perhaps it was because I misinterpreted our plan as military orders that needed to be carried out. Perhaps it was better than having no plan at all.

One beer followed another, and the empty bottles rattled and rolled at Danny's feet as we sped south. That was the only sound inside the car for the first hundred miles.

Then Danny spoke, "Go ahead, ask me questions. I know you're dying to."

"I don't know where to begin. I don't know what questions might be out of bounds. How about you just start talking? Tell me whatever you want me to know."

"Oh, that's pretty fucking clever! You put the ball in my hands, so I can't lash out at you for being too nosy or asking questions that are too invasive!"

"I'm not being clever, just careful. Do I have questions? Yes, lots of them. But I suspect this is a minefield, and I'm not going to get my legs blown off."

"Don't use any war metaphors for God's sake!" he screamed and then changed his tone to one I almost recognized. "Tell me, David, do you want to turn this fucking car around and go back?"

"I've been thinking about it."

"Don't do it! Please don't do it. I'll talk. I will! I promise. I need to talk. Maybe you can save me! I need somebody to save me. I need to talk, but I just don't know where to begin."

"Are you all right?"

"I'm fucking thirsty, but I can drink and talk at the same time. The army made me a master at multitasking. I can load my M16 while taking a piss!"

"Did that come in handy while in Vietnam?"

"Don't ask a question before you answer mine. Can you save me?"

"I'll listen, but I don't know anything about saving anybody. Start anyplace and stop when you've had enough. Maybe you can save yourself."

"That's psychobabble! I don't know how to save myself. Give me a starting point. Prime the pump. I need something to get me going. I'll take anything to get me started. I'll keep my responses short and stay somewhat in control. The beer has taken the edge off. I'm ready! I promise! Give me a word, just a word. I need to talk. I'll explode if I don't talk. Get me started! We'll build this conversation one fucking word at a time."

Danny sounded desperate in his begging for help. My mind sifted through a series of words that were possibilities, but I didn't know which ones would ignite a blast. I also didn't know how to connect the quiet kid I once knew to this loud and angry man.

I took a deep breath and began. "Recruiter," I said flatly with no emotion or suggestion of an expected response.

"Motherfucking lying bastard! He saw me coming. I was fresh meat for the grinder called war, just another sausage for the grill. I helped him to make his monthly quota. He helped me get a front row seat to the biggest show on the international stage. There was no applause! He was the first one I went to see when I got out. He wasn't there. He'd bought his own lie and died in one of the many bloody battles. I might have been there but never saw him. I saw way too much, but I never saw him… Next!"

"Joann."

"Bitch! Married the boy next door! She was pregnant when they tied the fucking knot. Seems as if my dream was like army boots. Fits anyone! He slipped right in and walked away. I got a letter from Niagara Falls. Honeymoon… Next!"

"Vietnam."

"Hell! Grass huts, rice paddies, water buffalos, heat, sweat, and chemical warfare pretending to be a color-coded herbicide. M16 rifles, hand grenades, helicopters with machine guns, and children lying dead in tank tracks. No sleep. No peace. No sense. Cheap sex behind the latrine… Next!"

"Liz."

"My big sister, Liz, had a flashback of sexual abuse. It all came back years after the assault. It came back in fucking detail! It was like being raped all over again. It was our mother's second husband. Dear Mommy never believed her.

Told her to keep her mouth shut! That's what put her in the hospital! Liz called me this morning. She quit her job before she even started! She's moving to Florida to live with our old friend, Pat, and make pizzas... Next!"

"Danny."

"Danny who? Danny what? Danny lost! Danny lost in speed! Fast women. Fast talk. Fast sex. Fast cars. Fast high. Fast everything! Get me there. Get me anywhere but get me there fast... ENOUGH! I can't play this word game anymore!" He dropped an empty bottle which hit another bottle, sending fractured pieces of glass across the floor. Then he slumped down into his seat and slept!

In his sleep he cried, tears rolling down cheeks tanned by hell's inferno. The breath of talking had blown over the hot embers locked inside him, bringing back the flames.

He was in pain! I thought I could help him and kept driving south.

Danny slept for hours, and when he woke, he insisted we stop at a bar just outside Lansdale, Pennsylvania. I did not want a beer but needed a break from the highway crowded with summer vacationers and big rig trucks. I dropped Danny off at a corner bar, saying I'd be back in a couple of hours. Then headed northwest a few miles to see if a girl I'd met in college was still home on summer break. I had her address and got there without getting lost. I had been lost in the car with Danny. Not because I didn't know the way to the beach, but because I didn't have a road map to saving him.

Terry was home and happy to see me. We talked for a long time about mutual college friends and the park where we used to hang out and drink cheap wine while munching on oversalted popcorn. The conversation took me back to Kansas and simpler times, uncluttered by big questions and concerns. I didn't mention the army or the situation with

Danny, who she'd met one New Year's Eve while visiting me in Syracuse.

Before I left to drag Danny from the bar, Terry asked if I had begun a job search yet.

"Not really. I've dropped off a couple completed applications but nothing that I'm excited about."

"In the Syracuse area?"

"Yes, but that's not where I want to be. I need to start my new life without being so tied to the past. I need a new beginning. Don't get me wrong, I've appreciated everything my yesterdays have given me and all the people I've been lucky enough to know along the way. It's all been great, but that's not what I need now. I'm done with the gray skies of Upstate New York. I love the snow but not so much of it. I want to be a train ride away from a big city. I want to discover what a total change would do for me as an artist. I want to be challenged by the unknown. I want adventure!"

"Sounds like you've made up your mind. Now all you have to do is find the right place."

"Do you think I'm crazy?"

"No crazier than you've always been."

"That's reassuring!"

"They're building a new high school in Lansdale, just a few miles from where you got off the turnpike. Stop by and check it out! Maybe they need an art teacher. This is a nice area. Philly is a half-hour away, and you've already got a friend here. I'm leaving for school soon, but I'll be back." Then she kissed me.

It was a kiss that promised more than friendship. It was a kiss that made me look for that new high school and forget that Danny was probably into his third beer at the bar where I'd left him.

I began to wonder how difficult it might be to get him out of the bar and into the car. I hoped he hadn't had any reason to interact with other customers, unleashing the vitriol I'd been exposed to earlier and causing a fight. The very thought of facing an uncomfortable situation helped me to delay the inevitable. I drove around Lansdale for a while and found the new high school Terry had talked about.

I turned into the parking lot and got out of the car, amazed at the size of the building. It was huge! I walked toward the front door without really thinking about anything other than what the art budget might be like for a school this large.

Before I knew it, I was walking up to the front door like I was a teacher going to work.

I pretended that was my reality and that a classroom filled with students was waiting for me. I could smell the paint the young artists hoped to use in creating something beautiful. I could hear the commotion as they took their seats and put the brushes on the table. Their conversation was alive with laughter as they made plans for the upcoming school dance and the football game with a local rival team. They were hanging their book bags on the back of their chairs and settling in as the first class of the day was about to start with a short lesson regarding the elements of design.

The Interview

I cupped my hands on either side of my face to stop the glare on the glass door and peeked into the new building. Suddenly, there was a friendly face on the other side bringing my dream to a sudden halt. He swung the door open and asked if he could help me in any way. I told him I was just being nosy but followed that up by saying I was interested in finding a job teaching art. He introduced himself as Mr. Kinter and offered to show me the art rooms.

As we walked through the halls, he gave me a little history of Lansdale and the school district. He was very proud of the school and said he had worked with the architect to design the art pod. The entire building had been created on the bases of pods, each of which had a different curricular focus.

It was a short tour because he had a meeting to attend, but I was thrilled to have had the chance to see the art rooms. As he walked me back to the front door, I thanked him for his time and the information he shared. He said that there was an opening and that the last round of interviews was about to happen across town at the central office. He encouraged me to hurry over and take a chance at being seen.

I had been a pretty task-oriented student and recalled all the great advice my professors had given me about interviews. They emphasized the importance of first impressions and recommended words to use and words not to use. They had been very specific regarding timeliness, professional appearance, and transcripts that I should have on hand. They recommended sitting up straight, speaking formally, and keeping good eye contact. They also said to keep a serious tone because there is nothing more serious than teaching America's children.

I was wearing torn blue jeans, a rock-and-roll T-shirt with Janis Joplin's image, and old sneakers. I was totally unprepared for an interview, but since I was also trying to delay meeting up with Danny, I drove to the central office that I had seen while trying to find the school. I completely expected to be turned away at first sight, but because someone else had not shown up for their scheduled appointment, they welcomed me in.

I sat in a large room facing five people who would be interviewing me. I explained that I'd just been discharged from the army and had been visiting a friend who said I should check out the new high school. I admitted I'd kind of stumbled into this unplanned interview, apologized for my appearance, thanked them for the opportunity, and waited for the first question.

"Fire away! I'm here and you're here, and I'm ready to dance," I said with a smile as if I had nothing to prove in the world.

At that point, the man I'd met at the high school came in and joined the interview team. Turns out, he was the head of the art department!

They asked me about my student teaching, past work experience, academic records, teaching philosophy, hobbies, interests, and dreams. Then they sent for my college transcripts and other pertinent information while requesting three names they could call as references. I was absolutely at ease through the entire process. I wasn't trying to get a job; I was trying to be me, a person that Terry had just reminded me of, a person who had been packed away in a uniform.

The group laughed at the impromptu aspects of the situation as they took my contact information. We shook hands and said goodbye with me thinking I'd never hear from them again. Days later when I called home to check in with my mother, she told me that I'd received a letter from the district office, notifying me that the job was mine if I wanted it. I was still in Virginia Beach with Danny and was shocked that my informal approach to an interview had resulted in a job offer. I was also thrilled that it was in an area that was close to Philadelphia, a city whose reputation for being a world-class arts center was known internationally. I was also fearful that the beginning salary might not be enough for me to eat regularly or afford a room. Despite all that, I called the district immediately and accepted their invitation to join the high school staff. I'd said yes to this offer without hesitation, feeling confident about being able to figure it out along the way.

When I shared the news with Danny, he said we could get an apartment together. I had my misgivings but agreed in order to afford a place to live. I also continued to believe that I could help Danny and thought that living together would increase the chances of that happening. I had known him before and after Vietnam and thought I could reconcile his two worlds.

I thought about the interview and how the district was taking a chance on a stranger who just walked in off the street. If they could do that, then it seemed necessary for me to risk having Danny as my roommate. I thought that providing Danny with a structured environment would have a stabilizing effect on him. I never dreamed that my exposure to his instability could have a deteriorating effect on my own steadiness.

Perhaps I overestimated my strength or underestimated the depth of his suffering. Either way, I had growing doubts about sharing an apartment with Danny.

The plan did, however, give me a foothold in a new state with a new job that I was very excited about.

As summer came to a close, my focus turned to the students that would be waiting for me. I reviewed the curriculum guide that I had been given and began to make rough drafts of lesson plans that would bring the curriculum to life within my classroom.

Creative ideas and anxiousness about the first day of school buried my fears regarding having Danny as my roommate. I was determined to be a teacher who would make a positive difference in my students' world and was grateful for this opportunity to teach.

The Job

Being a teacher is tough! There is nothing easy about this line of work. No amount of college degrees can possibly prepare even the brightest teacher wannabe for this important job. It requires life experiences and the desire to be a lifelong learner.

I went to a nationally known college that housed the National Teacher's Hall of Fame. I graduated with honors and was named the top graduate in my college yearbook. I was a member of the student senate and the head of several prominent college organizations. I was academically ready, but nothing prepared me more for being a high school teacher than being a drill sergeant in the army! It provided me with a context for all the theory I'd studied.

A teacher's world is filled with lesson plans, curriculum, instruction, assessments, rules, and regulations. But most of all, it is filled with students! Everything has to do with fostering a trusting positive relationship with those you are trying to move from point A to point B. It takes building a team, developing goals, and earning respect while you offer those around you the chance to earn your respect.

The young people who were put in my charge were like the soldiers I had been preparing for battle; only this time I was preparing them for college or jobs or life. I developed lessons, gave them materials and tools, and instructed them in their use. I wrote the objectives on the board and assigned tasks for them to practice their working knowledge. I created tests, tracked their growth, and I shared their progress with those having a vested interest.

It was an honorable service of duty, and I felt at home in this world. Every day that went by, I felt more confident that I was exactly where I was supposed to be and doing exactly what I was supposed to do.

I loved building a functioning community of learners! I loved the positive energy that was in the classroom, in the hallways, and every corner of the school. I also loved getting to know and working with other teachers and the parents we were partnering with. I loved the organization itself and its lofty goals to teach students how to think and build a better nation as well as a peaceful world for all people. I was in heaven!

That is why every day I was fearful that Danny would destroy my world! His behaviors were becoming more erratic and sometimes bordered on the bizarre. Despite everything, we moved forward with the plan. Terry's parents offered temporary floor space while I combed through the newspaper, searching for something permanent.

The search for an apartment was difficult. The Lansdale area was booming, and rental properties were rare and expensive. Even when one could be found, the renter often required at least a one-year lease and two months of rent in advance.

Danny and I went from checking out some large, bright, clean, air-conditioned and furnished places with tended grounds to settling on something we could afford. Our residence had a grungy narrow stairwell leading to a couple of bare bedrooms without locks, an empty kitchen, stained bath, and tiny living room. The living room looked like a place where people died in the middle of a food fight. It was in a questionable neighborhood but had a fan which Danny and I traded back and forth. It was cheap, so we signed the lease!

Over the next few months, we collected enough things from thrift shops and the side of the road to make it almost livable. My favorite side-of-the-road discovery was a kitchen table, around which we put four chairs that didn't match. I set my world globe on the center of the table and called the place home.

Danny soon lost interest in furnishing the apartment but still came home most nights following a day of work for a local contractor. Working seemed to help him stay more stable and enabled him to pay his half of the rent.

I found some old curtains, shades, and blinds at a Goodwill shop along with a couple of throw rugs. I also picked up two beds that somebody was throwing out! The beds got us both out of our sleeping bags and off the floor. The window treatments gave a little sense of privacy from the neighbor's prying eyes and helped reduce the echo in our mostly empty place. My mother sent sheets, pillows, and blankets, as well as two small lamps—one of which I had on a TV tray next to my bed.

I scrubbed everything down with bleach, hung up a couple of my paintings and a calendar. In low light, the place looked pretty good! At least that's what I told myself.

Danny continued to call our place the dump! I didn't try to change his mind. I had picked up on the fact that Danny could not be convinced of anything. If I said it was a beautiful day, he'd say it was going to rain. If I pointed out a colorful sunset, he'd say it was caused by radioactive dust. He wasn't satisfied unless he could poison everything around him. My up was his down, and I learned to avoid walking into the verbal traps he set for me. I could feel his anticipation of a comment I might make and so I said nothing. Most of the time, it was a very quiet place unless he could make all the rules. Sometimes I let him because I was looking for clues that would let me into the world he'd experienced.

He would regularly express the results of being in Nam but rarely shared what caused the anger, distrust, resentment, fear, and hate he filled the apartment with. Unfortunately, his dark mood overwhelmed all my attempts to make the apartment more attractive and livable. It was something I could not scrub away and so I tried to live with it like the old smelly couch left by the previous tenant that was too big to get out the door by myself.

The good news was my job and the energy from the students who brought me so much life and positivity. Their enthusiasm and creativity fed me far more than the peanut butter and jelly sandwiches I was surviving on along with popcorn and the occasional frozen pizza.

My job required as much strength and dedication as did the Drill Sergeant Academy, but I loved it and looked forward to each new day in the classroom. That is where I was the encourager and where I was encouraged.

I wrote a letter to Terry, telling her all about my students, their projects, the field trips we were taking, and the joy I was feeling about being a teacher. I didn't tell her anything about Danny. I didn't want her to worry about a problem she couldn't possibly solve. Her focus was on her studies, and that's exactly where I wanted it to stay. Besides, I still believed that I could help Danny the way the students were helping me. I tried to encourage him and talk with him and understand him, but there were many times when he saw me as the enemy and the target for his abuse.

He rarely missed an opportunity to use his sarcastic talent in berating my activities, my job, my interests, or lifestyle.

One evening while I was stretched across that old couch reading a book, he went on the attack.

"You lead a very exciting life! I can hardly keep track of all the women you keep bringing to this elegant palace! It's eight o'clock on a Friday night, and you're reading a fucking book. Let's get out of here! Let's go into the city. Let's go bar-hopping. Let's find a couple of babes and have a good time!"

"Great idea, but I've got exactly three dollars and only enough gas in my car to get me to school next week."

"What a pity! And you were such a bright boy with a college education and the one voted most likely to…what? I forget. Oh yeah, I remember. The one most likely to die of boredom before turning twenty-five. You're in the prime of your life, teacher boy, and you're reclining in this morgue with your nose glued in a book."

"It won't always be like this. I'm just starting out."

"I'm starting out right now," Danny said as he headed toward the door. "I'm going to that bar around the corner. Maybe I'll get lucky! Don't worry. I won't bring her back here. I wouldn't want to disturb your concentration." He slammed the door as he left.

I could have used a beer and a little time away from the apartment, but that wasn't possible. If I did have a couple of extra bucks, I wouldn't have chosen Danny's destination. I had gone in there once and the atmosphere and clientele didn't exactly make me want to stay. There were three pinball machines just inside the front door, a full-size pool table, a jukebox that only offered six musical choices, and a long sticky bar draped with very willing and available female companions. I'd seen enough places like this in small towns outside of army posts and had no desire to see another one.

I continued to read.

Danny came back the next day smelling like a dozen raw oysters and perfume that sold by the gallon.

I didn't bother to ask about his luck. I didn't want to know and could see by the expression on his face that he'd rather not say. He spent about an hour in the shower. When I heard him turn the water off, I left to go for a walk in the park.

I had finished my book and wasn't in the mood for any more of Danny's harassment. I didn't come back for hours, but when I did return, the apartment still smelled like Danny's experience of being lucky.

He slept.

I opened all the windows. I turned on the fan and tried to air out the place as much as possible. I wished that changing the root cause of the stench was as easy as opening windows and turning on a fan.

Big Mistake

My fears regarding having Danny as my roommate became more confirmed every single day. He was drinking more, smoking more, and driving drunk more often than not. Many times, I'd come into the blue haze of our modest apartment to find him surrounded by empty beer bottles and an ashtray heaped with ashes of multiple cigarettes and remnants of burned-out joints. Cannabis wasn't the only questionable substance he brought into the place. I found hard-core drugs in an ice tray in the freezer compartment of our refrigerator.

Sometimes what he ingested made him mellow and talkative, and sometimes he was aggressive, angry, and even scary. When he was mellow, he'd want to talk and fantasize, imagining all kinds of escapades we might have. During these moments, I rarely interrupted his storytelling. I just listened, hoping his make-believe world would help me understand his state of mind.

Danny was creative and no dummy, but he was troubled. At first, I didn't know the depths of those troubles, but I learned over time that his suffering was beyond my comprehension and possibly beyond my compassion and my tolerance.

His favorite thing was to play with my old world globe. He'd place it in the center of our table and give it a spin. Then he'd take another puff or gulp of whatever was his current fancy before pointing his finger and stabbing the globe to a halt.

"Let's see where this takes us," he'd say, slowly lifting his finger to reveal a destination.

Sometimes it was in China or Germany or a little-known village in South America. He always hoped it would be Paris, a place he believed was filled with beautiful women and adventure.

The uncovering of any site filled him with great excitement. He'd say, "You go east, and I'll go west. One year from today, we'll meet there, at noon, on that exact spot."

"What exact spot?"

"The biggest café on Main Street! Every city has a Main Street. All you have to do is look for the biggest café."

He'd go on and on about the fantastic adventures we'd have to tell each other when we'd meet. An evening spent around the spinning globe might last for many hours or all night. It would be filled with plots and subplots, sexy women and danger. It amazed me to hear Danny conjure up a tale out of nothing so filled with details that I'd almost believe it was real. Danny was at his best when he was in charge of creating his own reality.

He hated my saying anything about needing to get some sleep or even talking about something outside the globe game. Too often, I stayed with the table game at the expense of sleep just to keep him calm. This became impossible to sustain as my job demanded more and more of my attention and energy.

Often, the combination that Danny was breathing in and swallowing would keep him wide awake and agitated far into the night. If I said it was too late to play that game, he'd get loud and angry. He'd call me Sgt. Page and scream, "I don't have to take orders from you or anyone!"

Trying to keep things relatively quiet resulted in my suffering a severe lack of sleep. Nobody can teach if they're sleep deprived. Sometimes out of desperation, I'd sleep inside my car in the apartment parking lot. Danny found me there one morning and promised he'd do better. He didn't! He couldn't. He needed help!

I didn't call his mother because of what I'd witnessed on her porch that day we left for Virginia Beach. I didn't call his sister because I was unsure about her own emotional stability and didn't want to be the cause of a setback. I did reach out to local mental health services several times but was told they were overwhelmed and understaffed. They took my name and number but never called back.

Once around mid-December, I came home to find him spinning the globe faster and faster. He was spinning it so fast and so hard that he had to put his other hand on the base of the globe to anchor it in place.

"You're late!" he shouted. "I need you!"

"For what?"

"I can't let the globe stop spinning! I had to keep it going until you got back. It's been fucking hours! Now you're here to play the game. Put your finger on a spot and stop this thing. Hurry!"

I could tell it wasn't just marijuana or beer this time. He looked frenzied and kept yelling, "Stop it! Stop this fucking thing now! Now! Now!"

Just to end the yelling, I poked my finger at a random spot, stopping the ball from spinning.

"Get your finger out of there! Lift it off!" he screamed. "Where is it? Tell me exactly where we are. Tell me now. Tell me right now!"

I slowly lifted my finger while he repeated over and over, "Read it to me. Read it to me. Read it to me!"

"Vietnam," I whispered.

He went wild, turning over the table, sending the globe into the air, and beer bottles shooting like missiles everywhere. He jumped to his feet and ran out the door, screaming, "No! No! No!" I didn't see him for three days.

I heard a siren in the distance and wondered what had happened somewhere, but as it got louder and louder, I knew someone with authority was coming to my door.

By the time I'd picked up the bottles, washed out the ashtray, and opened the windows, there was knocking. I answered letting two policemen into the apartment. They said they received a call from a neighbor about a disturbance and questioned me about the noise.

"I'm so sorry to have bothered anybody and especially the two of you. As you can see," I said while pointing into the kitchen at the upside-down table, "I was trying to move some furniture and dropped the table."

They were great! They helped me set the table right side up and were on their way in minutes. I felt guilty lying to men in uniform. I also felt a sense of security knowing that help was available if Danny got completely out of control.

The second night that Danny was gone, I took a walk to see if that spool of wire he felt so connected to was still there. It was and I didn't know how I felt about that. I wanted him to be gone, but I couldn't afford the rent without him. I was also still hoping that I could help Danny in some way, but I didn't know how.

Eventually, Danny came home. I heard his key in the lock and looked up from the slice of frozen pizza I'd just taken out of the oven.

"Hungry?" I asked.

"Go fuck yourself!" was his response.

Soon, I smelled the familiar aroma of weed, and after about an hour, he joined me at the table where I was grading projects.

"What're you doing?" he asked as if no harsh words had been spoken.

I almost said working but caught myself at the last minute. "Just some school stuff."

He pushed an envelope across the table, saying, "Here's my share of this month's rent money." Then he left, saying he had to take care of some business.

I worried that the business he was taking care of was drug related. For weeks he hadn't been coming home covered with the grime of working in construction. I thought he wasn't working at all. Now that he coughed up the rent money, I suspected he'd found a more lucrative line of work—a line that gave him dirty money and clean hands. I didn't sleep much that night, which wasn't new. I didn't sleep much any night.

Unfortunately, sleep was something a first-year teacher can't do without. I had to be as completely prepared as possible, and even then the number of moment-by-moment classroom variables were enormous. I had to learn to survive the ever-changing world of a teacher and forgive myself for not knowing what I didn't know. I needed to learn how to adapt to the unexpected and build an arsenal of immediately accessible protocols to navigate challenging situations. This can't be done without sleep!

I wondered how Danny was able to handle the continuous sleep deprivation and asked him that question one midnight when he was going out for the third night in a row.

He shook a bottle of pills in my face, saying, "I've got a pocket full of sleep right here!"

I thought about calling the police, telling them about the drugs, and giving them Danny's license plate number along with a description of his car. I hoped they'd pick him up and stop this madness, but I feared how he'd respond to the uniforms, and I didn't want anyone to get shot.

I wondered whether there were other things he was hiding from me besides the drugs and alcohol. I tried to respect his privacy and didn't go into his room to investigate, even though I was tempted. No search of the spaces we shared ever revealed anything suspicious, but I had no idea what he might have stashed away in his car. I also kept thinking about a story Danny told me regarding witnessing a Vietcong fighter being chased down and run over by two soldiers in a jeep.

I sometimes thought he might be capable of using his car as a weapon. No matter where he was driving or under what road conditions, he drove too fast. He made frequent sharp turns, drifted through stop signs, and ignored traffic signals of any kind. He was often in the lane of oncoming cars and constantly drove with an unwarranted confidence.

I'd often take walks at night to get out of the apartment but always stayed close to buildings, trees, and lampposts that I could jump behind. I stayed alert and paid attention to headlights, especially when I heard any engine roar behind me. I tried to keep my imagination under control, but I also didn't want to be stupid.

I met a lot of soldiers in the army who had suffered war injuries, and when I'd ask how it happened, they'd often answer, "Being stupid!"

I was in a different kind of war and was not going to let stupidity take me down.

My military training became something I relied on. I had to see my old friend as a possible enemy as well as being someone who was hurting. I tried to stay alert at all times and made survival my number one concern. I continuously stayed aware of ways to escape and evade a conflict if it became necessary.

I also offered Danny opportunities to talk while expressing my support and encouragement when he seemed receptive. Most of the time, Danny was suspicious of anything I might do or say. He was angered and became outraged with resentment if he detected anything he determined to be of assistance or an act of kindness. Usually, I'd have to wait until he'd bring up a topic. Then I'd carefully nudge the direction of our words toward what I hoped could be discussed. Unfortunately, if he got a hint that this was a calculated move on my part, he'd say I was laying land mines and blow up in front of me.

His emotional outbursts were ugly, and the tension between us could last for days, paralyzing any attempt on my part to bring the conflict to a resolution. It took me a long time to see that paralysis was exactly what he aimed for. His moods and actions were premeditated, strategically placed armaments. They worked!

My defenses were weakened by his unconventional approach to this battle. I was reluctant to mount an attack being the proclaimed conscientious objector. I also did not want to be a prisoner of war and began looking for freedom beyond the confines of our apartment.

School

At first I questioned if I loved going to school because it was my escape from the craziness of our apartment, but soon, I began to see that teaching was giving me the opportunity to be completely myself. It gave me purpose. It gave me hope!

I was learning through teaching every single day. The students constantly asked challenging questions, and I felt obligated to answer them correctly and in a timely manner. I spent hours in the library making sure I was not shortchanging the kids.

Sometimes they'd sit in the library with me, and together we'd discover the truth. This was incredibly gratifying because I didn't pretend I knew it all! This opened up the door for them to show me how much they knew!

In my classroom, we'd share music and poetry and books and laughter. Sometimes I read plays to them while they were working on a drawing or painting. This spurred a conversation about initiating a monthly coffeehouse in the art department. The coffeehouse brought in parents who wanted to know why their kid was suddenly so interested in art. The students also wanted the art department to have a higher social status in the ranking of the curricular offerings, and together we developed a plan to make a special time for the department to show off all its creativity. We submitted the plan to the building principal, and to our delight, we got the go-ahead!

We transformed all the art rooms into galleries and spaces where student artists could demonstrate their skills. We baked all kinds of goodies and invited the entire school to come and see what we were up to. Everybody wore costumes and each teacher brought their class for a twenty-minute in-school field trip to experience this artistic happening. It was a huge success!

The guidance department was flooded with students requesting to schedule art classes for the next school year and visiting parents petitioned the school board to increase the number of art classes held at night for adult learners.

Suddenly, the art department became the cool place to be as well as my home. I felt safe and secure at school, physically as well as emotionally. I saw my future there. I knew I belonged there. I also knew I had to find a better place to put my head down at night.

My personal challenge was that I didn't want to give up on Danny. The kids in the high school reminded me of the Danny I knew when he was still in high school, before the Vietnam nightmare. My students were young and just beginning to stretch their wings to question and dream. This made me remember Danny's dreams, and I decided to put the same amount of time into supporting Danny as I had put into building up the art department. I knew this meant we'd have to engage in an honest talk, without games or drugs or booze. I dreaded the thought of it, and in some ways, I feared it. I tried waiting for the perfect moment, but that moment never came. I kept delaying the conversation but was positive it was as unavoidable as it was necessary.

Eventually, I promised myself that I'd confront Danny. I'd demand the long-needed talk, address issues, and make changes. I swore it would happen the very next time I saw him no matter the time, his condition, or mood.

When I heard him come into the apartment that one night, I was determined to bring up the entire situation with Danny. I was ready. I was more than ready! I needed him to know that I'd endured enough of his crap and that things had to change. I turned on a dim light and was standing in the living room when he closed the apartment door.

"You're up?" Danny said with surprise. "Want to play a game?"

"No games. I want to talk!"

"Talk to yourself. That way, you can say anything you want, and there's no one to disagree. I do that all the time! I'm my best company. Besides, I'm not in the mood for talking. I'm in the mood for a game."

"But it's necessary."

"Necessary for who? Certainly not for me!"

"For both of us, Danny! I'm worried about each of us. I don't know when I had the last good night's sleep. I never know what I'm going to find when I open up the apartment door. I'm worried about my job, and I'm worried about you."

"Me? Don't make me laugh. Nobody worries about me. If you had been worried about me, this conversation would have happened long ago." His words pissed me off! He seemed totally unaware of my concern for his well-being, but I was committed to staying calm and keeping him receptive to a talk.

"I tried long ago. I tried from the very beginning. I tried the day we left for Virginia Beach, and I've been trying ever since. It takes two to make a conversation. I have been talking to myself, and that ends now!"

"Make it a game and I'll consider playing."

"How, Danny? There's too much at stake. Talk to me! Is the Danny I knew still in there someplace?" I questioned while pointing at his head.

"That innocent and ignorant kid is long gone, you fool. He's never coming back."

"Where'd he go? Where have you been? Where are you now?"

"I don't think you really want to know!"

"Let me decide that! Talk! Explain! Share! Show me! Take me there! Where'd you go?"

"To hell, David! The kid you knew went to hell, and I'm still there! Do you want me to take you to hell? I can you know! I'm intimately familiar with every back road in the place. It will be a travel game that you'll never forget. I'll be your tour guide!"

"Tour guides have to talk! I will need some narrative to support what you show me along the way."

"Okay! It's a deal if it will shut you up. I won't give you the grand tour because it would be like living it all over again, and I can't do that. I'll give you the cheap tour bus version of hell, pointing out highlights from a safe distance. You won't even have to get off the bus while I draw your attention to particular points of interest. It's the best I can do! Are you up for the ride?"

"Do I need a ticket?"

"It's free for all veterans. It's a benefit my recruiter never told me about. Sit back and relax. This is going to require you to use some of your artistic creativity and imagination. Look out the window to your left and tell me what you see. There's a young private hoofing along the bomb-pocked road."

I sat on one of our old kitchen chairs, looking in the same direction that Danny was pointing, out an imaginary window.

"What do you see?"

"I see you, Danny," I guessed, hoping I'd played my part correctly. I was a tourist in a strange land, didn't know the rules of the game, and had no map. "You're wearing fatigues and walking alone on a dusty road."

"Yes! Very good! Oh, yes, I see me too!"

"Where are you going?"

"Into the village."

"What's its name?"

"It has no name. Lots of villages in Vietnam have no name. They come and go like the wind. It has no history of its own and is constructed from the remnants and pieces of larger villages that once had names. The people are reluctant to give these places a name because once they have a name, some asshole puts it on a map and then it becomes a target. It's not much more than a pile of rubbish that the locals sift through again and again, hoping to find a shred of something they could eat or use or trade or sell. The houses and local businesses are made from recycled war shit along with torn tarps, bamboo, and rope made from braided plastic bags."

"What kind of businesses?"

"All kinds! All the basic needs can be met here. If you want a wheel for your oxcart, just take a number. How about a head of cabbage? They're cheap! There is an army surplus store on every corner. You can build a jeep out of the assorted parts that are available for the right price. You can also acquire any number of venereal diseases for practically nothing."

"I don't see a village yet."

"You'll see it soon. It's just over the hill."

"You're moving pretty fast. Is there danger?"

"I don't care. I want somebody to shoot me."
"Are you carrying a rifle?"
"I'm only carrying my waist pack."
"What's in it?"
"All my money and the letter from Joann."
"What are you going to buy?"
"Don't be an idiot! I'm going to Madam Dung's Petting Zoo! What do you think I'm going to buy, a set of china for the mess tent? All the guys talk about this place and the services offered in the dim light of the canvas rooms."
"Have you been there before?"
"I've never been any place before. I was waiting!"
"I see."
"There it is, up there on the right with the tin roof and red curtain for a door. Don't you just love the name of this brothel? Three of the working girls are sitting in the shade, just outside. Do you see them?"
"I see them. Should I come in with you?"
"No! You pervert! Wait. Play with yourself if you have to."
"I think I'll just wait."
"I go in and ask for Madam Dung. Her English is a little shaky, but she gets by. She wants to see my money and then she shows me photographs of all the sexual acts that are offered and each one's cost. She goes into great financial detail about how you get one free for every two purchased and then taps her watch while explaining the time allowed for each experience. She tells me time is money and turns to get one of the regulars from the shade.
"I stop her and say no! I tell her I want a brand-new girl. At first she doesn't understand. I take a paper towel and drape it over the top of a vase on her dresser. I grasp the neck of it with my left hand and then poke my right index finger in,

tearing the paper towel. She laughs. She brings in the other girls and repeats the demonstration. They all laugh as she writes the price of a virgin on the back of her hand. It isn't cheap. I don't care! I'm thinking there is not one virgin left in all of Vietnam, but she sends them for a girl named Canh.

"I agree to the price as if I've ordered six pounds of choice beef. I'm led down a hallway made of curtains of all colors and into a small room that smells of perfume and spices. A few minutes later, Canh pulls the curtain open, steps in, bows, and closes the curtain before lying down next to me. She is fifteen at the most with big dark eyes and not a word of English.

"She undresses slowly, nervously holding the tattered material across herself, shyly waiting for me to act. I don't! I can't. She unbuttons my shirt, loosens my belt, and touches me in certain places as I'm sure she'd been taught.

"She is just another kid following orders, I think as I reach to hold her. I caress her. I touch her shiny dark hair. I pull her close to me. I am not the mad sex-crazed guy I was on the road. I am gentle. I am awkward. I am kind. She is warm. She is afraid. She is willing. I stop thinking. Instincts take control. It happens. I pay.

"Two days later, I am on that road. I carry my rifle. I do not want to get shot. I am eager but in control. I go over the hill and stop!"

"Why?"

"Can't you see? The village is gone! Madam Dung's Petting Zoo is gone! The girls in the shade are gone! Canh is gone!"

I looked up at Danny who was still staring out the window of our imaginary bus. His eyes were glassy and wet. He was absolutely still as he stared at the invisible village. Danny almost appeared to be frozen and unable to speak.

"Why did you go back to the village?"

"Don't pretend to be naïve! You're a big boy. You know why I went back. During the last second of a sexual act, the world stops spinning. In that moment, there is no war, and there is no ugliness. No fear! No anger! No orders! In that split second, there is only peace, and I wanted to feel it again. I wanted to know that it is possible."

"It is, Danny."

"Prove it," he said without emotion as he turned and walked to his room.

"See you at the bus stop tomorrow to continue the tour?" I asked.

"I can take it if you can," he responded before slowly closing his door.

Danny had let me see into his soul, and it hurt. He took me to Madame Dung's Petting Zoo for a reason. It was a scene I will never forget.

I went into my room to wait for sleep. It did not come. I wondered if I was now carrying some of Danny's burden. I wondered about the weight of the next site to be shared. I wondered about how much I could carry.

I had watched many war movies with my father. In some, a soldier carried his wounded comrade for miles in search of medical help. The soldier I was trying to rescue was not in my arms or on my back. He had placed a burden in my head, and I was beginning to bleed. I was filled with questions and no answers. The only positive thing was that Danny had talked. He had shared. It wasn't easy for him, and it wasn't easy for me, but a door that had been locked was now open.

I thought about Joann and Danny and Canh. I wondered which one of the girls Danny thought he was touching behind the curtain that day. I also wondered if Danny wondered if Canh became just another girl in the shade at the next transient village. Was she waiting like an old army boot for the next soldier to slip into? How many younger brothers and sisters was she feeding with the money she earned? How long before she would become a carrier of the diseases that require penicillin that she could not afford?

What if she had a baby? It was possible. It happens. Would it be a boy who would become a soldier? If so, on which side would he fight? If the child was a girl, would she work at another petting zoo?

I could not sleep. This first glimpse of hell was tattooed on my brain forever. Even though I'd only seen a secondhand version, it took a toll.

I wondered how long it had been since Danny slept without nightmares. Then I wondered if my father ever really slept after landing on Omaha Beach. I thought about the friends my father saw die in those shallow waters under a bullet-filled sky. I remembered how important it was to him that I learn how to swim. He taught me. I can still hear him yelling, "Keep your head down! Keep your head down!"

Being a Coward

When Danny returned the following night, I was sitting in my assigned seat next to the window, ready for the next stop on our journey. Danny came in rolling his car's heavy oversize spare tire on its chromed steel wheel and parked it upright next to my seat.

"I thought our pretend bus needed at least one wheel for symbolic reasons."

"Okay, if you think it helps tell the story!"

"Oh, I do! I love symbolism and things that spin fascinate me. They go round and round and round and end up in the same spot."

"What kind of things?"

"Normal everyday things, like wheels and globes and clocks and people."

"Now that we have our symbolic representation to help us with the next turn of events, let's get things rolling."

"I have to say that you surprise me, David. I didn't think you'd board the bus for the next scenic attraction. Yesterday's visit to the petting zoo was a lot to take in."

"It was! Visiting the petting zoo wasn't exactly a stroll in the park, but I didn't expect it to be. I don't imagine it was easy for you to live it or to share it. I only got a rerun of that spectacle, and it left me speechless."

"Good! That's a big part of hell. It leaves you unable to fully put it into words."

"Talk of being surprised, I am surprised too. I didn't think you'd continue the tour. Revisiting any part of the war zone must bring it all back."

"Don't kid yourself! I don't have to bring anything back. It's always with me every second of every day. The only thing that's different is this time, I'm letting someone else see it. Did you enjoy the view?"

"Not at all! I hated it. It was sad and disgusting. It made me aware of the possibility of other terrors beyond what you shared, things that I didn't know existed."

"I suppose it can go in one of two ways. It can expose a larger picture, or it can make you blind! Where should we go today?"

"You're the tour guide. You know what needs to be seen. I'm just a passenger here. I'll go where you take me."

"For a drill sergeant, you're giving me a lot of power."

"I trust you to use it wisely."

"Don't be so sure! Yesterday's ride was a little bumpy! Are you bruised?"

"I can handle a rough ride as long as it's a round trip. I wasn't expecting anything smooth."

"Look straight ahead. Look at the big window in the front of the bus. What do you see?"

"Nothing in particular!"

"You're missing the details, David. Look up there in the center. Look in the rearview mirror and see me."

"You, when?"

"Me when I learned I was going to Vietnam!"

"Okay. I recognize that kid, so young and vulnerable!"

"And stupid! Don't forget stupid," he added with anger. "I was scared shitless! I thought I'd be stateside in an air-conditioned office, not in a jungle on the other side of the world. I thought I'd be surrounded by typewriters, adding machines, and filing cabinets, not snakes, constant rain, and low-flying helicopters that never take me out of there. I learned how to fire a weapon but thought I'd be chasing papers, not another young soldier with a different uniform. I was going to use the army to get a degree. I never imagined the army was going to use me!"

"It's the chance you took when you enlisted."

"It's a fucking chance I never bargained for. I didn't understand. I was a fool. I got my orders. I got on a plane. I got to Hanoi. I got on a truck. I got to my base. I got sick to my stomach."

"Along with thousands of others!"

"But I was scared!"

"They were all scared."

"Not like me! I saw them laughing in the mess hall. I saw them playing basketball on the tarmac."

"Coping mechanisms! They were scared to death!"

"Were you ever scared? I know you didn't go to Nam, but were you ever scared?"

"I was scared ten thousand times. I was scared I'd end up in Vietnam. I was scared I wouldn't make my father proud. I was scared I would fail out of the Drill Sergeant Academy, but most of all, I was scared I might not have taught the men in my platoon how to stay alive."

"Did you ever think of running away? Going AWOL?"

"I wouldn't let myself think about that, but lots of guys thought about it and some did it."

"I thought about it, but it was too late. Before I understood I was going to Nam, I was there! I think they plan it that way. Did you know anybody who deserted?"

"Yes! Late one night while on leave in Lake Charles, Louisiana, a friend of mine made that decision."

"Tell me about it."

"Am I in the driver's seat now?"

"Just once around the block! You're not qualified or certified to give the hell tour. Just tell me about that guy."

"I'd just witnessed an ugly fight in a seedy bar on Main Street and was trying to put some distance between that bar and me before the military police arrived. It was just after midnight when I wandered into a park behind an elementary school and found a guy I'd met in Advanced Infantry Training. He was sitting on a swing, and when he looked up, the lights from a passing car flickered across his face. And I recognized him.

"I sat on the swing next to him and asked what he was doing. We both began to swing, stretching our legs out and then pulling them back as we hunched our bodies forward. I said it was funny that we were two grown men pretending to be children. He said it was tragic because we were really children pretending to be grown men.

"As we swung higher and higher, he said he had received his orders for Nam and wasn't going to go! He told me he was scared and that he didn't want to die. He asked if I thought he was a coward."

"What'd you say to him?"

"I said I didn't know. I also begged him to go back on base and find the chaplain to talk to. I told him it was too big a decision to make alone. He was so very scared. He could barely talk. As I was telling him the possible consequences of running, he jumped off the swing, midair. I heard him land somewhere out there in the dark."

"Did he go to Nam? Did he go AWOL? Did he end up dead or in jail?"

"I don't know. I couldn't see a damned thing. I always hoped he'd broken his leg in the fall and ended up in a state-side hospital."

"What's the moral of that fucking story?"

"The moral is: We're all going to be scared at one point or another. It comes with being alive!"

"That's bullshit, Sgt. Page. You don't know shit about being scared!"

"You're wrong, Danny, but I'm not the one who's supposed to be doing the talking. I'm not taking us on a side trip to view my shit. If being scared is the next stop on the tour, take me there!"

"I was trying to delay our departure. I hate seeing myself in the mirror!"

"Sometimes getting a good look at yourself can be helpful."

"Not if you don't recognize that person! I look and see a stranger. I see someone pretending to be me."

"Stay with the topic! I believe you were taking me someplace where you were scared."

"One night in Nam, I was on patrol. I was guarding the munitions stored in a metal Quonset hut. There was supposed to be two of us, but we were understaffed because of a recent offensive. It was late and I was tired. I was trying to stay awake, alert, and ready for anything. We'd been warned that the enemy was near and that they were desperate for weapons and ammo. Every time I took a step, I thought I heard someone behind me. I'd swing around, rifle in hand, crouching low to the ground, ready to be attacked."

"And?"

"And no one was there. After the fifth time, out of breath and frightened, I ducked into the shadows and lit a cigarette. I had learned to smoke in the army. It calmed my nerves. Within two months, I was another one of those three-packs-a-day guys.

"As soon as I lit the match, a shot rang out, and a bullet grazed my unbuckled helmet, spinning it off my head. No one came running. No alarms went off. No lights lit the camp. I laid there shaking as the cigarette I'd dropped set the dried weeds on fire. Sgt. Malory came out of the dark strutting across the field and emptied a helmet of water over my head. He said he was more than a marksman. He said he was the best sharpshooter in the battalion and that if I ever lit a match while on duty again, he might forget how to aim.

"He ordered me to stamp out the fire and return to my post.

"Before walking away, he said, 'I know you're scared, son. We're all scared, but now you're scared with a load of shit in your pants! Things can always be worse!'

"That's the kind of scared I've been since getting out of the army! I'm afraid I'm a born coward. I'm not in Nam anymore, but I'm scared of everything. I used to be afraid of dying. Now I'm afraid of living! I have a load of shit in my pants every day!"

"Maybe you brought Nam home with you!"

"Don't say that! Don't ever say that."

"Is it too close to the truth?"

"Vietnam was supposed to be a tour of duty, not a scavenger hunt. I didn't want to bring anything home."

"But you did!"

"I told you not to ever say that. Not fucking ever!" Danny shouted as he ran back to his room and slammed the door.

In many ways, I found this stop on the tour more heartbreaking than the first stop. In his own way, he'd shown me the ugliest souvenir any soldier could carry home from battle, bone-deep memories of the war itself. All Danny's fears, regrets, and sins were on exhibit, and he knew I'd seen them. Now I was his mirror reflecting everything he hated. He had been hiding all this in booze, drugs, and even games. But a game of his own making took me to the hot blue flame that burned within him. I was scorched by the heat, but Danny was on fire.

I questioned whether to allow the tour to continue. It was hard to watch, and I could see how difficult it was for Danny to share. I thought about rolling away the tire and letting him return to the globe. But at least he was talking, and I hoped that something good would come from sharing the trauma that was crippling his life.

My father talked about his war constantly. Every time we were alone together, the war was with us. I knew all the battles and where they took place. His words had taken me to Africa, Sicily, and Normandy. I knew where Sal had been blown out of a foxhole and how Frank lost his arm. I knew each class of heavy military-ranged artillery weapons that launched munitions far beyond the power of infantry firearms. Guns, howitzers, and mortars were part of my vocabulary by the time I was ten. He had carefully described the chaos when the mess tent was suddenly under attack and how they went three days without food. He recalled hours of being crammed into one of a hundred trucks bouncing through bomb craters in a mile-long convoy heading to a battle from a battle. When his truck stopped, he discovered the quiet soldier he was talking to had been dead the entire time. He talked of an all-night march in soaking-wet boots and collapsing with the fevers of malaria.

He repeated those stories and many others over and over to the point where I could have told them with almost as much detail. There was one story in particular that always left him unable to continue. My father was there when Gen. Patton berated two soldiers and slapped one for suffering from battle fatigue and shell shock, two things that four-star asshole refused to acknowledge as being real.

I'll never know what effect telling those stories had on my father, but hearing them from childhood on had a profound effect on me. The stories left scars as if I had been in the battle.

I grew up wanting peace and believing that peace was possible as well as necessary.

The kids in the neighborhood where I grew up pretended every stick was a sword or a gun. I didn't think that was so unusual and guessed this might be the case in every backyard across America and around the world.

I questioned why every kid wanted a BB gun for Christmas, and more importantly I wanted to know why they used those guns to shoot small birds and torment stray cats. I did not want a BB gun for Christmas or at any other time. They reminded me of my father's stories, even when they were only used to knock tin cans off the fence. That game seemed like an innocent introduction to a much darker sport, and I didn't want to play.

I hoped to find pencils, paints, and art materials under the Christmas tree and was thrilled to find them there. My mother did all the Christmas shopping, which sometimes included things like a microscope or chemistry set.

Toys can determine and reinforce a direction in a child's life. I often wondered what Danny played with when he was a child and why he could only express himself within the context of a game. I never asked him that question for fear he'd close down the only opening I had for communication of any kind.

Since playing a game was something he considered safe turf, I was willing to go wherever he'd take me. That didn't mean that I was unaware of the danger.

End of the Tour

The next night, I took my seat on the bus and waited for Danny to come home. An hour passed and then two. I didn't think he'd take me on another sightseeing ride and used the time to grade projects and enter the grades in my book. Then he walked in and stood in the doorway.

"You're a little late for our tour. The other people got tired of waiting and left," I said as he entered.

"You know there are no other people. This was a private tour and now it's over."

"It can't be over. I know you've got lots more to share."

"It's over when I say it's over! The tour became something else, something I had to stop."

"What do you think it became?"

"It became an archeological dig! You were excavating my mind, and it gave me a migraine."

"I was hoping that shedding a little light in those dark corners would relieve a little pressure and give you some peace."

"You were wrong! Maybe it was you who wanted a little peace. Maybe everything has been about you and not me at all. I think you were doing to me just what you're doing to your fucking students."

"And what the hell is that?"

Danny charged into the apartment, grabbed all my paperwork, and threw it around the room while yelling, "You were assessing my progress and writing down my grade in your imaginary book! You were making a determination regarding my stability and worthiness. You were grading my sanity!"

"You've hit a nerve, fucker! First of all, I don't do things to my students. I do things for my students! Secondly, I'm not your teacher. I'm a fellow student, a classmate in the school of life trying to learn how to survive!"

"Well, this particular field site is closed to further study. The processing and recording of the remains has come to an end. I'm conducting my own study, and you are the focal point of this investigation."

"Why? What do you expect to find?"

"Maybe if I sift through the details, I'll discover why you didn't go to Nam instead of me."

"Is that what this is all about? Do you wish I'd been there instead of you?"

"I wish anybody had been there instead of me, but yes, you in particular! I'd like to be the one with the grade book assessing your level of success! I'd like to put a fucking *F* on your report card. Zero class participation. No assignment turned in on time. Attitude, shit! Disruptive! Arrogant! No focus! No feelings. No future!"

"Wow! I have only wanted the very best for you! I didn't have a clue that you hated me so much. I thought you were suffering!"

"I've been suffering you, you idiot! I hate your confidence! I hate your fucking fortitude and good fortune. I hate your success! I hate that I haven't been able to beat you in this game."

"I didn't even know it was a game."

"Maybe that's why you win, you bastard. If you don't know you're playing, you can't lose! Why didn't I fucking think of that?"

"So the tour goes in the toilet?"

"It was shit anyway. Give it a flush and get a plunger to force it down. I don't want to see any floaters in the bowl the next time I take a piss."

"So if the bus is parked, where do we go from here?"

"I don't know about you but I'm going out for a beer."

I jumped up, slammed the apartment door shut, and turned to face him, showing a side of me I'd never let him see before.

"I'm afraid your fucking beer will have to wait until you pick up and neatly stack every single paper you threw. All this paperwork is my, *get ready for it*, WORK! It's not just what I do. It's who I am, and you're not going to stop me from being the best of that person ever again." I stepped closer, attempting to make him understand things that I was only just beginning to understand myself.

"You brought up the key to a locked door during the last stop on the tour, and I'm turning it! Here's the truth. Have I ever been frightened? You bet your fucking ass! I was frightened that I wouldn't know how to find myself. I had no clue how to become this man. I had no mentor, no model to pattern my behavior after. I searched and struggled and clawed my way uphill to be what stands in front of you today. No college degree, no Drill Sergeant Academy, no one gave me a road map to being me. There were obstacles and hellholes I had to face. There were huge questions and missing pieces to the puzzle of my life. I had to fucking handcraft connecting tissue on my own to complete the picture."

I stepped even closer and, confidently in my deepest voice, whispered, "I am sorry you went to hell. I'm sorry that anybody had to go to war. I'm sorry I couldn't help you, but right now you'll be sorry if you don't carefully pick up and neatly stack every paper!"

"Is that an order?"

"It's a very strong suggestion," I said, inches from his face.

"That sounded like an order to me. Do you think you can enforce it?"

"I know I can!"

We stood there nose to nose in silence. I did not even blink. Eventually, he broke the stare down and gathered everything together, leaving my student's work on the bus seat. Danny sped out the door and down the steps, punching holes in the drywall of the stairwell as he descended.

I started searching for another place to live that night. It was obvious the punches were really meant for me. I went through the newspaper looking for cheap apartments and found that nothing was cheap enough. Then I looked for a room, thinking I'd buy a hot plate and eat canned soup. Even those places were too expensive, and they wanted two month's rent in advance.

Eventually, I looked beyond the Lansdale area and started to make some phone calls. I didn't have any luck, but it felt good to be actively trying to make a change. It felt good to stop letting his sickness be in control. I needed Danny to know he wasn't the only one who was carrying some anger.

I remembered a time when I was about fourteen, and I was angry with my father. My mother had spent a week with her siblings in Massachusetts and called to say she was ready to be picked up. My father asked me to ride along. He even suggested we could bring a tent and camp at a lake in the

Adirondacks for a couple of nights. I jumped at the chance and helped pack the car with everything, including fishing rods and firewood. I was very excited and couldn't wait to get on the road. He told war stories all the way to the lake, and like always, I listened. I tried to tell him about the things that were happening in my life but gave up. My life didn't capture his interest. I hoped that things would change when we got to the lake and were sitting around the campfire or fishing.

I was wrong! He stared into the flames which triggered memories of the First Division's capturing of Aachen in October of 1944. This story took hours, so the next day when we were supposed to be fishing, he slept.

I was angry and didn't say another word until we picked up my mother in Massachusetts. I don't think he even noticed.

The Uniform

Though an army uniform was no longer my everyday outfit, it still hung pressed and ready in my closet. I was in the army reserves, and for one weekend every month and two weeks each summer, it was a reminder of other duties.

While at my next army reserve meeting, I met with an officer to privately talk about what I had been observing and dealing with in regard to my recently discharged roommate and veteran.

He listened carefully about Danny's wild mood swings, his drug use, and his violence. He listened as if he'd heard it a thousand times before, shaking his head periodically and even tearing up over the bus tour. When I asked what I could do, he advised me to move out and not leave a forwarding address.

"But I want to help him."

"I'm sure you do. I'm swamped with calls from mothers and wives, siblings, and friends with stories like the one you shared with me. The government didn't see this coming, at least not to this magnitude. It's everywhere and to varying degrees. Hospital rooms, prisons, and sidewalks are filling up with young men and women who can't start a new life because their old one was too traumatic. It can't be silenced.

It talks to them twenty-four hours a day. They are only partially here. Mostly, they're back in action.

"What can I do? He's going to hurt himself or somebody!"

"He's the one that has to reach out. Not you! It's the law! He's a veteran. There are services available. Not enough but there are some. He has to want the help! He has to complete the proper forms, and he must submit them to the appropriate office. You can't do a damned thing! You're not even a blood relative. No one is going to listen to you. With luck, he'll get picked up for some minor crime and fall into the system through a back door. Can't you talk to him?"

"I've tried! He's way out there and getting farther every day! I'm walking on thin ice with every step."

"Would he hurt you?"

"I don't know."

"Move out! If you can't move out right away, find a way to be out of the apartment as often as possible until you can leave permanently. I can't help you or Danny. Posttraumatic stress disorder, PTSD for short, is real. It's deadly and it's everywhere! It's nothing new. It's been around as long as there's been war. They used to expect soldiers to just get over it! Of course, many of them didn't. Nobody just gets over being in a war!

"Understand that you are in danger, David! Until you can get away, be sure not to let him know you're afraid. Don't let him think he has power over you."

I had learned this to be true during active duty and was glad to have the reminder. Even though I was discouraged regarding finding help for Danny, I felt better after sharing the situation. I was determined to get out before things got worse.

Months later, when returning to the apartment from two weeks with the reserves, I found Danny sitting at the table, spinning the globe.

"Are you wearing that fucking uniform?" he yelled without looking up.

"You know I have to wear it for the meetings and our drills. Don't worry, I'm changing," I said while walking into my bedroom.

I pulled off the uniform, leaving it on the bed. I was anxious to see Danny's state of mind and if there had been any change during my absence.

"Oh, I'm not worrying. I took three anti-worry pills. They're like anti-tank guns, blowing the hell out of whatever I might worry about."

"Three?" I questioned as I walked back into the room, wearing something I knew he'd find acceptable.

"I used to take one and then two, and now I have to take three before my head gets quiet. I like the peace. I like calm waters."

"I do too."

"Let's sit with the globe. We haven't played that game in a while."

"Do you think we could talk a little while the waters are calm?"

"Your constant need to talk worries me. Are you having some kind of problem?"

"I think you have the problem, and your problem has become mine. I'm giving it back. I think it has to do with the war, and I think you need professional help."

"What the fuck do you know about war? You ducked that bullet!"

"I know about the war my father was in and what it did to him and our family."

"Your father fought in World War II from Africa to Europe. I've heard his stories. He walked away with only a few fragments of shrapnel in his ass. Big fucking deal! Mr. Chuck Page is one of the kindest, most even-tempered men I've ever met. Nothing rattles him! If that's the result of war, give me an armored truckload."

"Not all people who have PTSD suffer the same symptoms."

"PTSD? I'm impressed! You must be spending time in the library, you nosy misguided bastard! What were your father's symptoms, obsessive smiles and too much goodwill?"

"My father came home from the war unable to have an opinion, be angry, think on his own, or do anything without an order. He took a job driving a city bus because he needed to wear a uniform! He lived by way of the bus routes that kept him on track and on a schedule."

"Give me an example of how his supposed PTSD negatively affected you or your family. Just one! I'm getting tired of this talk and very thirsty."

"I can give you a thousand of them!"

"Just one! I'm running out of patience and I'm oh so very dry!"

"When I was in second grade—"

"Oh, fuck! How long is this story going to take?"

"When I was in second grade, the teacher was talking about family and asked if anyone knew their father's full name. With excitement, I quickly raised my hand. When she pointed at me, I stood up and shouted, 'Jesus Christ Chuck!'"

"Why in hell would you say that?"

"Because that is the only way my mother could get him to do anything. She had to grab his attention and issue a strong order to even get him to go out in the backyard and play catch with me. She said it so often, I thought it was his name."

"You're more pathetic than I imagined."

"I was just a kid and she had to become the captain and take charge! Believe me, that wasn't in her nature or in her plan. It became her duty if the family was going to stay together. She had met him before the war and married him when he returned from Europe. She had no idea he wouldn't be the same person."

"How'd it feel to have your mother order your father to pay attention to you?"

"I felt like shit! I felt like a burden, unwanted and ashamed."

"Poor baby! What's this little bedtime story have to do with me?"

"If you can't see the connection, I can't help you."

"No one asked you to!"

"I thought it was my duty."

"Your duty is to shut up and play!"

Danny pulled the globe to him and began to make it spin.

"Go ahead, Danny. Make the world go around if all that's left is the game."

"Do you realize that my spinning the globe causes the tides?"

"No! I didn't know that," I answered, watching him smile at the oceans and seas and great lakes of the world.

His eyes flashed back and forth to catch a glimpse of the next section of earth's waterways before they spun out of view and out of his head, like the story about my father. "It's true. I have a great responsibility here," he said very slowly as he gently gave the globe another turn. "The average human body is 60 percent water. The tide affects everybody and everything that has a little bit of moisture in it. Even each and every single teardrop is affected by the tidal pull. I have to be careful!"

We played the game in slow motion that night. It might have been the result of the three pills or his way of stretching the game beyond my bedtime. The globe spun incrementally. He hardly blinked and took one breath for every three of mine. Then he stood without a word and stumbled down the hall, where he fell into his bed and sleep.

I stayed at the table watching the globe slowly come to a stop. I wondered at that moment about what might be happening around the world. How high was the tide? Were there any ships lost at sea? Were there any survivors?

Then I went to my room, but it took a long time for sleep to come. Just like most nights, Danny would yell out in his sleep. Usually, it was just one word at a time. "Fire!" was among the words yelled most often along with "Help!" This particular night, he kept yelling, "I'm drowning! I'm drowning! I'm drowning!"

Finally sleep came to me, forcing the globe to stop spinning in my head. I dreamed of riding on the city bus with my father. My mother made him take me to work with him periodically, thinking it would be good if we spent some time together. I watched him greet every stranger with his big smile, warm hello, and conversation as I sat silently in the seat behind him, seeing myself in his rearview mirror crying.

I woke to a series of loud noises and banging on the apartment door. A deep determined voice was yelling, "Open up! It's the police!"

The banging might have been going on for a while, but I thought it was Danny in the next room or a dream. I sat up, trying to make sense of the situation but couldn't. It was the continuous flushing of the toilet that brought me to my feet and my eyes to the clock which flashed 3:30 a.m. I went out to the hallway and saw Danny run from our only bathroom into his room.

I opened the apartment door, sporting only my underwear. Three officers burst in, the door banging against the wall. I was barely awake and stood there silently, trying to convince myself that I was having a nightmare.

"Where's the shit!" one officer yelled.

"What shit?" I questioned.

Then it hit me. Suddenly, I was totally awake and knew what Danny had flushed down the toilet. They pushed a formal-looking document into my hands and searched through every room, pulling out couch cushions and turning over mattresses. They yanked clothes from closets, hauled out old suitcases, and turned over cardboard boxes of schoolwork; their contents fanning out across the floor like a paper rug.

Then they were gone in a huff, leaving every closet door open, every drawer pulled to the floor, every pillowcase inside out! Everything was naked and as exposed as I felt in my underwear. I stood in the middle of the mess, wondering if this raid was going to be the headline news in the local paper.

I balled up the document and threw it in Danny's face as he entered the room, yelling, "This is your fault, asshole!"

"What do you mean? I'm the hero here! I'm the one that made the sacrifice!"

"What the fuck are you talking about? You're no fucking hero!"

"Hey, teacher boy. Let me give you a lesson! They didn't find any shit here, did they? That makes me a hero! It cost me a bundle to save your ass. There'll be some happy rats in the sewer tonight! Now clean up this shit!" he ordered as if being the hero put him in charge.

The longer Danny talked, the more I suspected he probably shoved as much down his throat as he did down the toilet. He was beyond reachable. His eyes were dilated and face, flushed.

"I've got to go to work!" he shouted, bolting out the door and down the steps.

I heard the roar of his car and the squeal of the tires as he sped away. I hoped the cops were following him, but they were not.

I had never been so angry in my entire life, and I hated to be angry. Anger steals a person's sense of logic and distorts reality. I wasn't thinking clearly, but I did clean everything up. I threw Danny's crap into his room and packed everything of mine. Each time I filled a box or container or suitcase, I'd carry it out to my car. I didn't own much, but my car was too small for what little I did have. Soon, I understood I had to make more than one trip. Then as the adrenalin wore off, I realized I had no place to go. I also remembered that my name was on the lease along with Danny's and that there were six more weeks till the end of that contract. I didn't want to stay, but I also didn't want to lose the down money that would be coming my way. I stayed!

I dragged a few things back to the apartment and got ready for school, determined to stick it out and glad that in the chaos, the globe had been broken into eight pieces. I left them on Danny's pillow and then sat down on the edge of my bed to collect myself for a few minutes before facing my students. Unfortunately, I closed my eyes.

At 10:15 a.m., I jumped up, freaking out and practically doing a free fall down the stairs before racing to the high school, running across the parking lot, and then casually walking into my third period class as if I'd just stepped out into the hall for a moment.

All the students were quietly working on their projects. They had taken roll as I had trained them to do and written questions on the board for me to address whenever I was available. There was a note on my desk from a student who had taken attendance in homeroom and sent it to the main office. The note read, "Have a nice day, Mr. Page." I could have cried!

In the Drill Sergeant Academy, we were taught that leadership begins with sharing all responsibilities so that the mission continues to be addressed no matter who might be missing in action. Now I knew it was true. Luckily, there was no mention of the previous night's incident in the newspaper. I had a splitting headache, but I still had my job!

The very next day, I brought cookies in for every class and reminded them that if I could not be seen, they were to alert the teacher in the next room.

I made a promise to myself that I would never again let Danny's behaviors interfere with my duties as a teacher. Those kids were my mission! Not Danny. I didn't want any student to be at risk or go unsupervised ever again. I also wanted an administrator to go looking for me in case I was bleeding to death back in my apartment.

I'm not completely sure how I managed to get through the day. I suspect it was because of the positive energy I felt from my students. I tried to hide my feelings behind smiles and pretended it was business as usual, but some things can't be disguised.

Three times before the final bell rang, I had a student ask if I was all right. It was like having them say I love you.

As I slowly and cautiously drove out of the school parking lot, I wished that Danny could feel that kind of love and see that kind of beauty, but I knew that was impossible. He was blind to anything beautiful and hated himself too much to be loved. My mind wandered back to that particular spring break and the roads we took to find sunshine in the middle of winter. I thought about Liz and how she'd been violated, received help, and was able to go forward. I thought about Rita who found she was going in the wrong direction and turned her life around. I thought about myself and the challenges as well as opportunities I'd encountered along the way.

I thought about Danny. Oh, how I wished him crystal-blue waters, warm temperatures, and a sandy shore under a bright yellow sun.

When I got to our apartment, I was exhausted! Climbing up the stairs was almost impossible. I didn't eat a thing. Sleep was all I wanted. Danny was not home, and I was glad to be alone and free from any of his antics. I would not have had the energy or will to engage in any interaction. I fell into bed fully dressed and slept as if my life depended on it.

When I did wake, I was incredibly hungry but not for any of the leftovers in the refrigerator. I tried to find something tolerable but decided I'd drive to a local diner and blow the ten bucks I'd been saving for an emergency. I felt desperate enough to call this an emergency.

I ordered meatloaf with mashed potatoes and gravy, green beans, and a fresh salad. It came with a buttered roll, but that wasn't enough. I ordered a piece of apple pie and hot coffee. I hadn't eaten like that in months!

It felt good to be full! I enjoyed placing the order and having the feast brought to my table. The entire meal took me an hour to consume. When I asked for the bill, I was told that the parents of one of my students had paid for everything and even left the waitress a tip. They had not identified themselves but had told the waitress it was for making a difference in their son's life.

It was the best part of the meal!

Overboard

Danny used glue and tape to put the globe back together and placed it in the center of the kitchen table. The clear tape let all the details show through, including the results of the recent man-made earthquake in our apartment. Now it wobbled as it turned.

I stayed away from the apartment most of the time. I'd accepted a role in a play that was being produced at a local theater, and gratefully, there were lots of rehearsals. I also remained after school to sponsor an art club and hung out with a few teachers who had become my friends. Sometimes I'd spend Sundays at Terry's parents' house, where there was always a standing invitation for dinner.

I was developing a real life for myself in Pennsylvania and had people to share my life with. There were parties to attend and conversations that didn't involve globes or games. I went out on dates. I played tennis at a local park. I met other art teachers, and we exchanged lesson plans and creative ideas. I also became an active member of the Teacher's Union and worked toward better pay and benefits.

When I did have to return to the apartment, I did it with great trepidation.

Danny didn't like not knowing where I was. I never divulged my whereabouts or plans for fear he'd show up.

One late Friday night, I quietly came into the darkened apartment intending to go directly to bed and was startled by Danny lighting a match in the kitchen. He held the match to the end of his cigarette and sucked in the heat. The flame mixed with the swirling smoke as his glazed eyes met mine.

When the match burned out, he spoke with only the glow from a distant streetlight filtering through the venetian blinds to catch our features. "I don't see you much anymore," he said with a mouth full of smoke that lasted the length of the sentence. "You know, Uncle Sam raped me! He fucked me up as much at my stepfather fucked Liz. It took a lot of professionals to put her back together! You are my tape and glue. Where've you been?"

"I've been busy!"

"Too busy for an old friend?"

"Are we friends, Danny?"

"Sure! We've been around the globe a hundred times together," he said while stumbling with his words. "Remember the time we met up in Paris after arriving from opposite directions? We dropped our backpacks and sat at that café, drinking beer and sharing all the stories of our separate travels to get to that particular spot. It was noon, just like we planned. I saw you coming and laughed out loud before calling your name. I told you about a lover I had in Marseille. She looked a lot like Rita. Beautiful Rita! I called her Star. You told me about those bandits who tried to steal your pack on that freighter in the Atlantic. You threw one of them overboard as I recall. Am I going overboard, friend?"

"Our lease is up and I'm moving on."

"Without me?"

"Yes! I need a place of my own. Terry's grandfather helped me find half of an old farmhouse out in the country where rents are cheaper. Her father is lending me his pickup truck to move my stuff."

"Sounds like a plan has been made while my back was turned! Why? We have a life here!"

"The plan was necessary and long overdue. I can't go on never knowing if the cops are going to bust down the door and drag us both out of here. This isn't living. It's barely existing. I doubt if Brenda Star could have figured out this mess."

"You know, David, not all plans work out. I'm an expert on plans that don't work out. I could write a book about it."

"I believe you could. I've always believed you could do great things, even when you were a kid in high school. You're smart and creative and capable of building a wonderful future!"

"Get real, David! That kid you knew is dead! What you see is a walking corpse. When I was given the order to use a flamethrower on that grass hut, I died! I died along with the three little children who ran out on fire. I watched all of our dreams go up in flames. I can still smell the flesh burning off their faces. I don't deserve to have a dream or a plan or a future. Maybe nobody does. Brenda Star should have investigated that fucking mess!"

"Did you ever tell anyone about what happened?"

"No! That was going to be the third stop on the bus tour, but I couldn't do it."

"So nobody knows what you saw?"

"You mean, what I did! Again, the answer is no! In the madness of bomb blasts and rifle fire and machine guns from helicopters and screaming friends and foes, I followed fucking orders. That's all there is to tell! I followed orders!"

"There are counselors that can—"

"Fuck counselors! They can't make me unsee what I've seen or undo what I've done. I can't talk to anyone."

"You talked to me. I listened!"

"I inflicted my memories on you. My words were weapons. They were meant to hurt you. I shot you with my nightmares. Didn't you feel the pain?"

"Yes, Danny, I felt the pain. It was horrible. I'll never forget any of it."

"I wanted to tell my army recruiter when I got back to the states and then kill the bastard. But he was already dead. Just like the song says, 'I can't get no satisfaction!'"

"But—"

"But nothing! You were a drill sergeant. You taught us how to use the weapons of war, the tools of the trade. You still do, one weekend a month and two weeks every summer. How do you stand yourself? When you have taught a kid to follow orders without knowing what those orders are, how do you sleep at night?"

"By trying to build a better world!"

"Try harder! The world's a fucking mess. Read the newspaper, watch the news on television, and listen to it on the radio. There's another war in the making before the last one is put to rest."

"I'm not saying everything is always perfect! I'm not blind. I see the ugly shit you're focused on, but there's more to life than that."

"Not in my life," Danny whispered as he spun the globe.

It wobbled on its axis, slowly turning in his blue breath.

"The tide is going out. Do you feel it?"

"No, Danny."

"It is! I felt it this afternoon and walked down to visit my brother."

"Your brother?"

"Yes. He's been leaning against that telephone pole for a year."

"What'd your brother have to say?"

"Nothing!"

"Nothing?"

"He's gone."

"Gone where?"

"Overboard, I guess."

Danny grabbed the globe with both hands, slowly crushing it beyond repair, asking, "Do you hear the people screaming, friend?" He held the hot end of his cigarette over the remains of France, stubbing it out in Paris before pushing back his chair and going to his room.

I sat there for a few minutes, processing everything that had been said, grateful that it was out in the open. Finally after months of planning and preparations, Danny knew I was leaving and that he wasn't coming with me. I had been keeping this secret for months. It felt like I'd been holding my breath underwater for a long swim. Now I could breathe! The need for sleep suddenly swept over me. I went to bed and prayed for all those who make orders and take orders and break orders.

Hours later, I was awakened, but I didn't know by what. I was on my back, listening to the sound of the old fan in the window when I opened my eyes. Danny was standing over me, holding that huge spare tire with its chrome-steel wheel, high over his head with both arms straight up and spread wide so his hands could grasp the circle's edge. I stiffened but did not move. I didn't even breathe.

"I could have killed you," Danny said without moving a muscle.

"Why didn't you?"

"I wanted you to see it coming."

"Well, now I've seen it," I said without emotion, slowly rolling over onto my side and closing my eyes.

"Games and the talk around the table can be very revealing. I've been listening and want to tell you what I heard."

"And what is that?"

"Your father couldn't let himself get close to you. He was afraid he'd lose you like he lost his brothers-in-arms in the war." Danny stood there for at least two very long minutes as if he was waiting to be dismissed.

"It's late, Danny. The game is over!" I was sweating through the sheets wondering if my sweat was affected by the tide.

Finally, he dropped his weapon! It grazed my pillow on its way to the floor where it landed flat with a loud and substantial thud after pushing over my makeshift nightstand and crushing the lamp.

"If I were you, I'd sleep with a machete under your pillow. I always do!"

"I'm not afraid of the dark," I said with my eyes still closed and practically pissing myself.

"I am," Danny said softly as he left me alone totally, absolutely, entirely drenched and wide awake.

Unable to move, I lay there in the dark listening to Danny gathering belongings from his closet and dragging them down the stairs. The last sounds I heard were the repetitive brushing of a broom, the pulling shut of the apartment door, and then the roar of his car fading into the distance.

I still couldn't move. My entire life was randomly rerunning in my head.

I thought about that army friend who jumped off the swing in the middle of the night and wondered if he'd made the right choice.

I thought about my hometown, parades, and bicycling down Main Street under the elms.

I thought about my sisters, friends, and girls I'd dated.

I thought about college and the army.

I thought about Mr. Mike's, Jake, and the music.

I thought about Danny, Liz, Rita, and spring break.

I thought about my mother and my father dancing.

I thought about the students I've taught.

I thought about Terry and all the experiences I'd put in my memory bank.

Then I thought I heard the cash register drawer slide open and the bell ring!

I moved out at daybreak.

Danny's room was empty. He'd packed up clothes and bedding as well as towels and other things from the bathroom. He had swept everything clean! Danny took all that was his, except for the circular weapon on the floor of my room, the key to the apartment, and the stories he left in my care.

Crossing the State Line

Terry and our sons were still asleep in the car. I was beginning to feel the need for a little stretch and a break from memories. I wanted to stop but knew that stopping would wake everyone. That would result in diaper changes, trips to the restroom, the inevitable cup of coffee, and the end of the story.

I wish I could say that it was my diligent focus on the wet road that kept me awake, but it was the long-overdue dealing with memories that was keeping me alert. I was dredging up the past and using the sludge to build a temporary structure to house yesterday's ghosts. It worked perfectly! I was absolutely there in time and space. I was walking through buildings that had been torn down ages ago, feeling old fears and struggling with a reality that had come and gone.

It amazed me that a chance encounter on a sidewalk could prompt a recall of such enormity. The details were incredible. Sights, sounds, smells, and specific words to certain conversations were all clamoring for my attention.

I wondered if that was exactly what Danny was experiencing when he got home from Nam. I wondered if posttraumatic stress disorder was contagious and if I had caught it.

I pulled off Route 81 and onto the Pennsylvania turnpike, remembering making the same move with Danny's

Camaro years earlier. He was asleep at the time while I was contemplating a U-turn that would have changed everything.

I love my life, my wife, my kids, and my job. The plan to head for Virginia Beach had worked for me. Danny wasn't ready. In many ways, he wasn't even there.

I continued to let individual events be played out before me as I drove my family through the storm. I could feel the impact of the wind periodically pushing against the car and see debris blowing past my headlights. It was similar to the inside of my brain!

Stories around the spinning globe, sobering walks down Main Street, the bus tour to hell, and Madam Dung's Petting Zoo were back in my head after being silenced for years.

I drove the last two hours in torrential rain. It was dark and very difficult to see. Even with the wipers on the highest setting, I couldn't clear away the downpour fast enough.

No one had stirred in the car, and I was wide awake, praying there'd be no interruptions. I was desperate to keep my place in the story and be able to put it in a safe spot with its proper ending.

As I exited the highway onto the familiar country roads leading to our home, I tried to search the far reaches of my mind to find anything that needed to be dealt with or was left unsaid.

It wasn't until I brought the car to a stop and turned off the lights, there in the middle of night, with the rain slowly transitioning to a sprinkle then a mist and then nothing at all, that the last words of the story came to me.

I lowered the driver's side window, looked out into the dark, and spoke, "I forgive you, Dad."

The End

Epilogue

Danny was not awarded the Purple Heart, the distinguished decoration for those who have been wounded or killed while serving in the US armed forces. My father received that medal, but not for the deeper wounds I saw.

Danny is not disfigured. None of his blood was spilled on foreign soil. He can hear and see. He still has all his limbs. He walks on two legs. No bullet is or ever was imbedded in his body. To the rest of the world, he appears unscathed by the ravages of war, but not to me!

I knew him before the war. I knew him before those arms picked up and carried the war home with him. I knew him when his head was filled with dreams and not nightmares. I knew him before the disfiguring invisible scars tied him to a place and time he never wanted to be and could not escape from.

Danny was my roommate during his first year after his service. I witnessed his limping through the present while being crippled by the past. He could barely hold a job because his arms were already filled with things he couldn't put down.

He was unable to touch his dreams because they were out of reach.

He was one of the walking dead who couldn't be buried because he was still alive.

Danny didn't receive the Purple Heart, so this book will have to do. I knew I'd have to write this the moment he shared the weight of what he was carrying. He had all of Vietnam on his back, his knees buckled, and he went down.

Danny was unable to handle the past or the future and manufactured a third alternative. He invented games, and they became his life where he could be in charge of all the rules. His reality was supported by drugs, alcohol, and fantasies.

I knew him before and after the war. I bridged both worlds and tried to help.

I could not but maybe this book can help others!

I don't believe any war ever really ends. Some people find a way to move on, but to a degree, the war always moves with them.

I did not go to Vietnam, but Danny brought the war home to me. That was the context for the lesson he taught, and I barely survived its teaching. It was the same instruction my father had given me but delivered in an entirely different way.

Now I've shared the wounds I saw and sustained from my position on those battlefields. I've pulled them out like shrapnel from my own flesh. I've laid them in the open and made order of the mess. I will not pack them up and zip the military backpack shut, confining the experience to the dark. I will live with them in the light of day. I will talk about them. I will cherish them like rare things forged in hell that brave soldiers brought back for me to see and benefit from!

I still hear Danny screaming in the night, but I go back to sleep with the hope that the more people grasp the reality of war, the greater the chance of peace!

I close my eyes and see that freckled-faced boy who was and still is my friend, wherever he is.

War is something that no one should live with or die from.

About the Author

D. C. Page has often been called a Renaissance man. His life is filled with artistic expression and productivity. He writes, paints, performs, and encourages others to reach their full potential. Trained in the arts, education, administration, and leadership, David has traveled all over the country, sharing his love of creative efforts. In his free time, David can be found hiking with his wife in the Swiss Alps, Italian Dolomites, or anywhere there is an adventure to be had or beautiful scene to paint.

Printed in the USA
CPSIA information can be obtained
at www.ICGtesting.com
LVHW091618081124
796097LV00001B/181